Economic Advice
and Executive Policy

edited by
Werner Sichel

Economic Advice and Executive Policy

Recommendations from Past Members of the Council of Economic Advisers

PRAEGER SPECIAL STUDIES IN U.S. ECONOMIC, SOCIAL, AND POLITICAL ISSUES

Praeger Publishers   New York   London

Library of Congress Cataloging in Publication Data

Main entry under title:

Economic advice and executive policy.

(Praeger special studies in U.S. economic, social,
and political issues)
    Includes index.
    1. United States—Economic policy—1945-1960—
Addresses, essays, lectures. 2. United States—
Economic policy—1961-   —Addresses, essays,
lectures. I. Sichel, Werner. II. United States.
Council of Economic Advisers.
HC106.7.E317   1978   330.9'73'092   77-7807
ISBN 0-03-022381-4

PRAEGER SPECIAL STUDIES
200 Park Avenue, New York, N.Y., 10017, U.S.A.

Published in the United States of America in 1978
by Praeger Publishers,
A Division of Holt, Rinehart and Winston, CBS, Inc.

89   038   987654321

© 1978 by Praeger Publishers

Printed in the United States of America

I wish to dedicate this volume of essays by members
of the President's Council of Economic Advisers to
my Council of all kinds of good advice:
my wife, Beatrice
my son, Larry
my daughter, Linda

ACKNOWLEDGMENTS

The essays included in this book were originally prepared for presentation in the Seminar in Economics series at Western Michigan University during the 1976–77 academic year.

I am grateful to the many individuals who helped me with the organization of this seminar and the preparation of this volume. Advice and assistance were provided by many members of the Department of Economics, particularly by Myron Ross and Eric Duesing. Financial support, a necessary condition to carry out a project such as this, was arranged through the good offices of Dean Cornelius Loew, Associate Dean Tilman Cothran, and Professor Raymond Zelder, chairman of the Department of Economics.

Several other people were indispensable. Cress Strand, Deborah Hochstetler, and Christine Truckey did much of the typing, the retyping, and all the sundry chores associated with the administration of the seminar and the preparation of the manuscript. Jeanne Parsons, administrative aide to Dr. Marina v. N. Whitman, was very helpful to me.

I am very thankful to all of these people, but my greatest debt, of course is to the authors whose papers appear in this volume. They visited Western Michigan University and delivered a version of the essay found in this book when their opportunity cost was obviously very high. The trade-off that they were willing to make—educating students and colleagues, for higher monetary earnings or leisure—can only be explained in terms of their altruistic spirit, their missionary zeal, and the rather high income tax bracket in which they find themselves.

Last, I sincerely thank my wife, Beatrice, my daughter, Linda, and my son, Larry, for their usual patience and understanding when I spent my time with the seminar and the preparation of this book rather than with them.

CONTENTS

Economic Advice
and Executive Policy

INTRODUCTION
Werner Sichel

In 1946 the 79th Congress of the United States enacted Public Law 304, better known as the Employment Act. The act included (1) a declaration by the Congress that it is the policy of the United States to foster "useful employment opportunities," (2) a mandate for an annual economic report by the president of the United States, (3) the establishment of a Joint Economic Committee of the Congress, and (4) the establishment of a Council of Economic Advisers (CEA) to the president of the United States.

This book focuses on the last of these four provisions. It is not a study of the council's activities or an evaluation of their successes and failures; rather, it recognizes the resource value of those who have served on the CEA and presents some of their views and advice.

The president's Council of Economic Advisers is composed of three members who are appointed by the president, by and with the advice and consent of the Senate. One of the members is designated the chairman of the CEA. The 1946 Employment Act states in part that the duties and functions of the council include:

> (1) to assist and advise the President in the preparation of the Economic Report;
> (2) to gather timely and authoritative information concerning economic developments and economic trends, both current and prospective, to analyze and interpret such information in the light of the policy declared in [the employment policy section of the Act] for the purpose of determining whether such developments and trends are interfering or are likely to interfere, with the achievement of such policy, and to compile and submit to the President studies relating to such developments and trends;

(3) to appraise the various programs and activities of the Federal Government in the light of the policy declared in [the employment policy section of the Act] for the purpose of determining the extent to which such programs and activities are contributing, and the extent to which they are not contributing, to the achievement of such policy and to make recommendations to the President with respect thereto;

(4) to develop and recommend to the President national economic policies to foster and promote free competitive enterprise, to avoid economic fluctuations or to diminish the effects thereof, and to maintain employment, production, and purchasing power;

(5) to make and furnish such studies, reports thereon, and recommendations with respect to matters of Federal economic policy and legislation as the President may request.

This book takes the view that economists who have attained the status in the economics profession—by virtue of their training, scholarship, and experience—to be invited to serve as members of the council and who have then performed the duties and functions enumerated in the act are among the most eminently qualified people to analyze our economic problems and to offer advice.

In the 31 years that the council has existed only 35 persons have served on it. A few of those are now dead, so that at the present time this elite group numbers just over 30. Six of them have contributed to this volume. As seems only fitting, three are from each side of the aisle. Paul W. McCracken served Republican administrations from December 1956 to January 1959 and from February 1969 to December 1971. Hendrik S. Houthakker served a Republican administration from February 1969 to July 1971. Marina v. N. Whitman, the third to serve a Republican administration, held the office from March 1972 to August 1973. The contributors to this volume who served Democratic administrations are Roy Blough, who was a member of the council from June 1950 to August 1952; James Tobin, who served from January 1961 to July 1962; and James S. Duesenberry, who was on the council from February 1966 to June 1968.

As most readers will recognize, all six of our contributors are vigorous and active practicing economists today. Only Roy Blough is retired from his university affiliation, but he compensates for that by doing more writing and consulting.

The topics that are covered by the contributors to this volume range quite widely, but complement each other well. Each is concerned with today's economic problems and attempts to analyze them by seeing what we can learn from the past.

Paul W. McCracken provides the reader with an insider's view of the office of council chairman. He describes the unique placement of the

CEA and its substantial influence for such a minuscule agency. He points out how close the CEA is to the president of the United States, a feature that is supported by the fact that the council chairman reports directly to the president. McCracken reminds the reader that most government agencies as well as cabinet positions have a "particularized constituency" that they cater to, but that in contrast the CEA, by virtue of its placement and the way that the discipline of economics examines problems, takes the general-welfare point of view.

McCracken, a very pragmatic practitioner of economic policy making, discusses how difficult it is for the White House and the CEA to control monetary and fiscal policy; the Federal Reserve and Congress may simply not cooperate. In fact, McCracken points out, the CEA spends a great deal of its time on micro as opposed to macro policy questions.

Looking ahead, McCracken, like virtually all of our authors in this volume, is very concerned with the lack of capital formation in the United States. While Tobin advises policies to stimulate spending in general and Duesenberry would like to see federal budget surpluses, McCracken's remedy lies in providing greater profits for business firms, which he claims are much lower than they appear to be. In his discussion of the dual problems of inflation and unemployment, McCracken speaks out against, as we would expect, direct controls, but contrary to the image that most people have of economists associated with the Republican party, he favors direct public employment in the presence of minimum wage laws for the hard-core unemployed. Without great elaboration, McCracken makes many trenchant remarks and provides some important insights.

Roy Blough draws upon his 50 years of experience as a professional economist to interpret U.S. economic developments since the 1920s and to examine extant problems and their possible solutions. He feels strongly that the preservation of democratic government and of economic freedom in this country depends upon our maintaining the economic objectives of low unemployment, stable prices, and economic growth. He believes that government intervention should be minimized but doesn't think that many self-correcting opportunities exist in our "big business" and "big labor" environment. Likewise, he is in favor of using the package of fiscal and monetary policy but feels that there is little prospect of correcting the economic dilemma of the 1970s through these means alone. He therefore advocates—in direct contrast to McCracken—an incomes policy. However, Blough and McCracken are in agreement that if wages can be set low enough, excessive unemployment should be met by direct public employment.

Possibly the most controversial recommendation that Blough makes is in the sphere of federal government planning. He goes well beyond the planning concept as discussed by Marina v. N. Whitman, who merely wants some contingency plans to reduce the nation's vulnerability. Blough wants to fight unemployment and inflation through government planning. He believes that good government planning can prevent sectoral shortages and bottlenecks in the supply of labor, plant capacity, and raw materials. He also advocates planning to deal with the proposed "New International Economic Order," which demands an economic restructuring that will permit the acceptance of more imports of manufactured products to the United States from the less developed countries of the third world.

Hendrik S. Houthakker, in contrast to our other contributors, focuses primarily on just one area of major concern—the international monetary system. He presents a careful analysis of the international monetary developments during a period of about 25 years that led to the collapse of the Bretton Woods agreement in August 1971. He then brings the reader right down to the present time, appraises the current situation, and offers advice for the future.

One has to be impressed with the very honest and forthright analysis that Houthakker offers. He lived the events and is able to interject descriptions of the feelings of particular personalities—philosophical as well as political—who caused certain major decisions to be made.

Houthakker takes the reader from the late 1940s when the dollar was very strong through the long period of the late 1950s and 60s when the dollar was overvalued. He explains the unrealistic exchange value, how devaluation of the dollar was repeatedly rejected, and how the United States attempted to compensate by increasing liquidity through swap arrangements, special drawing rights, and Eurodollars. Also, how the United States, in order to keep its balance of payments deficits under control, adopted restrictions on international payments and increased its protectionist policy.

Houthakker believes that the world after Bretton Woods is learning to live with "managed floating" but would like to see a continued search for "an international monetary system more flexible than Bretton Woods, yet capable of providing comparable stability."

The fourth contributor to this volume, James S. Duesenberry, believes that the greatest analytical error that economists have made during the decades since World War II is to fail to appreciate the vulnerability of the United States and other market-oriented economies to inflation. He explains that it doesn't take much to start or to accelerate an inflation. He recognizes the supply-side problems and that well before a nation approaches full utilization of its resources, certain bottlenecks put upward pressure on prices.

Duesenberry displays a very pragmatic attitude toward stabilization policy. He suggests that we are not able to control the economy with great precision. Policy instruments work with long lags, and this means that we have to forecast. Most of our forecasts are in the right direction—so it is better to act than to "wait and see"—but surely we should expect forecasting errors.

As to what policy to pursue, Duesenberry sees a fiscalist-monetarist convergence of views. He finds monetary policy to be very unsatisfactory as an active stabilization policy but recognizes that it does have important effects on the economy. He advocates a fiscal policy that would provide some budget surpluses in the early 1980s to combat the shortfall in investment forecast for that period. Cautioning against using short-term stimulus policies that will make long-run problems more difficult to solve, he favors temporary tax reductions and public works over the next few years as opposed to permanent tax reductions and expenditure programs.

The only woman to have ever served as a member of the CEA, Marina v. N. Whitman, discusses several major economic problems that face the United States today. She suggests alternative explanations for them and accordingly examines different prescriptions for what to do to solve them.

The problem that she refers to as the "centerpiece" is stagflation, the simultaneous occurrence of recession and inflation. She explains the competing explanations of (1) inflationary expectations left over from a previous prosperous period and (2) enormous cost increases in some key sectors that reverberate throughout the economy. She points out that if the first is correct, then a slow approach that will squeeze out the inflationary expectation is in order. However, if the second explanation is right, the government can aggressively stimulate the economy without much danger that the cost increases will occur again.

Whitman utilizes the same level-headed approach in discussing other extant problems. Addressing unemployment per se, she examines the pros and cons of direct versus indirect job creation and analyzes their different effects on the growth of labor productivity and therefore on real wages. When discussing the anticipated problem of capital shortage, she reminds the reader that these forecasts are made on the assumption that capital-output ratios will remain the same and that this is, of course, not necessarily the case. She also deals with the issue of output allocation between public and private goods, the need for government planning in a world of uncertainty, and the issue of what the U.S. response should be to the changing nature of international interdependence.

Finally, Whitman brings together all of the difficult issues that she raises in her essay into two major overriding questions. The first is whether the United States can maintain a democratic political environment and at the same time engage in rational economic policy making.

And the second is whether the neutral "liberal" international economic system that we are used to can survive in an environment where the less developed countries of the world are pressing for a meaningful international redistribution of world income.

In the last essay in this volume, James Tobin presents a penetrating analysis of the American economy in 1977 that is in sharp contrast to that of our other contributors, Republicans and Democrats alike. Whereas Duesenberry found inflation to be of paramount concern, Tobin suggests that the policy of the Ford administration and the Federal Reserve under the Carter administration is aimed at a very slow decrease of inflation, the elimination of which takes precedence over every other objective. He is concerned that the Federal Reserve will choke off the recovery by increasing the money supply too slowly, thus tightening credit and increasing interest rates.

Tobin presents a Keynesian diagnosis of the current situation, explaining that it is "too little spending" that prevents the United States from reaching "full recovery"—that it is "deficient effective demand" that causes Americans to live with too high an unemployment rate, too low a growth rate, and not enough investment. He strikes out at those who say that there really isn't anything wrong with the U.S. economy; that employment has hit record highs and that much of the unemployment in an environment of high unemployment compensation, food stamps, and increased participation in the labor force of women and teenagers is really voluntary. Tobin is unwilling to accept their "market evidence" based upon the fact that wages are not falling. He reminds the reader of what Keynes had recognized in the 1930s—namely, that wage and price patterns are typically very sticky.

The brief summaries and comments provided in this introduction were intended to whet the reader's appetite. I am confident that after reading the six essays that appear in the remainder of this book, the reader will agree with my contention that past members of the CEA are indeed important resources for us to tap when we need advice. Once again, I wish to thank the contributors to this volume for participating in my Seminar in Economics at Western Michigan University. The essays in this book are essentially and substantively the lectures that they presented to the seminar.

2

AN ELDER STATESMAN'S
ADVICE TO A
CEA CHAIRMAN
Paul W. McCracken

My most immediate advice to the chairman of the Council of Economic Advisers is that he fix firmly in his mind a passage from the Old Testament—namely, Ecclesiastes 3:1–8. For readers who are a bit wobbly in matters of theological literature, Ecclesiastes 3 is the source of the statement: "To everything there is a season . . . a time to be born and a time to die." Then follows a dozen other opposites. Now if the Employment Act of 1946 had been signed by King Solomon instead of by President Harry Truman, I have no doubt that the prophet would have worked his list from 13 up to 14 by adding, "and, finally, a time to become Chairman of the Council of Economic Advisers and a time to get out." Just what kind of sermons could have been developed out of such an added text must remain a mystery, and mankind will simply have to get along as best it can without ever having the mystery resolved.

There are, of course, many dimensions to success in this position. One is for the chairman to do a good job, but that seems too obvious to belabor. A very important requirement is to play the economic rhythm correctly. This means taking the job when therapy to straighten out an economic problem has been applied but before it has taken hold, or before people perceive that it has taken hold, and to leave before the next mess comes along, which in the ineluctable rhythm of the economic cosmos is apt to occur. Now, entering at the right juncture is apt to be somewhat automatic. An administration whose lot it is to deploy those policies needed to cool an inflation, for example, is apt to get turned out at the polls, letting the next occupant of that spacious office at the south-west corner of the Executive Office Building's third floor come in to take credit for the better economy whose improvement really reflects policies of his departed predecessors.

The problem is to disembark at the right time. This is difficult. Certainly to get out when economic trends are going awry would be interpreted as being fired for failure. And when finally some of these trends are going in the right direction for a change, it seems a pity not to stay around and enjoy life for awhile. As I read the history of this remarkable little agency, however, its chairmen who have been deemed to be relatively successful have been those who were shrewd enough to see the delights of a return to academe and to disembark "too soon"—that is, before the next economic storm blew in.

Most who have had some experience at writing know that an essay sometimes goes in directions that the writer did not quite anticipate at the outset. That is true for me in this case also. I had expected to make a few prologomenous comments about what might be called operational matters, and then go on to policy. As this essay took shape, these observations about operational and institutional matters began to loom somewhat larger than I had expected. This is not amiss, however, because when economists discuss policy they need to have some awareness of the institutional framework within which these processes must work themselves out. To say that altering the policy parameters of our equation system in specified ways will give us our optimum result is to leave discussion of these matters at a quite disembodied level.

Suppose that we begin with a question. Why is it worth giving advice to the chairman of the Council of Economic Advisers about his job? There are many officials in protocol-conscious Washington who at the innumerable dinners in that town would outrank our CEA chairman. Why not a collection of essays on advice to one or another of these "more important" people, such as the secretary of commerce, just to take a for instance. (After all, it is his department that produces the national-income and other data that are so frequently used by economics practitioners.) Moreover, in the federal establishment, the CEA as an agency is hardly large enough to be of even petty-cash-fund proportions. It has a total personnel of about 50 if at full strength, and a budget of $1.7 million. That is not really a minimally respectable figure in Washington—well below the $2.3 million for the Office of the Special Representative for Trade Negotiations, and about one-fifth of the budget allotted to the Office of Telecommunications Policy. Now, foreign trade and telecommunications policies are certainly important enough, probably more important than most people realize, but hardly in the same league with the importance to us of a healthy economy generally.

Yet it is clear that this position of chairman of the CEA is an important one. This book contains six essays centered on this job, but the position is also considered to be peculiarly important by far more important people than academic economists (whose attitude on these matters would, in any case, be suspected of reflecting a degree of parochiality). When the CEA chairman gives a major address or statement to a committee of the Congress, the press gives it wide coverage. When a new person is appointed, it is front-page news. In the summer of 1976, newspapers gave far more attention to then Governor Jimmy Carter's economic adviser and the possible future CEA chairman, if the governor's next address were to be 1600 Pennsylvania Avenue, than to potential people for other positions to which protocol allocates a higher rank.

What accounts for the influence of an agency of such miniscule size? There are, I believe, a few things to say about this, and it is important for a chairman and for the rest of us to keep them in mind, and for a new chairman to ponder them. For one thing the chairman reports directly to the president, and those who have direct access to the Oval Room also have influence laterally in government. Since this point is self-evident, it needs no belaboring—except that anything that might significantly attenuate this direct relationship between the president and his economic adviser would convert the Council of Economic Advisers from a quite influential agency to another of the numerous Washington groups frenetically engaged in much ado about nothing.

There is another aspect of this point, however, which is not always realized. Almost any proposed program cuts across departmental lines. Energy programs, for example, are of concern to the Departments of Interior, Commerce, and State as well as to the Federal Energy Administration. Welfare programs are of concern obviously to Health, Education, and Welfare (HEW), but the Department of Agriculture will also be interested, and certainly the Office of Management and the Budget has a proper concern about the cost. The Council of Economic Advisers plays an underappreciated and useful role in the coordination of these activities, and it is not unusual when walking down the hallway toward the office door of the CEA chairman to see cabinet officers entering or leaving his office. This "lateral" influence on programs and policy derives in part from the fact that the CEA and its chairman are close to the president. These consultations range from ad hoc task forces to structures for continuing consultation—for example, the Economic Policy Board, which meets each morning at 8. Indeed, amidst the jockeying for personal influence and position that always goes on in Washington, the chairman should recognize the importance of effective and continuing consultation with others also concerned with general economic policy—for example, the secretary of the treasury, the director of the Office of Management and the Budget, the Federal Reserve chairman, and others.

A second source of influence on policy by the CEA and its chairman is that it looks at economic policies from the same vantage point as the president—namely, the general interest. This is not as obvious as may at first seem to be the case. The fact is that most of the cabinet members have their own particularized constituencies to which they are expected to be responsive. It is the job of the secretary of Housing and Urban Development (HUD) to be concerned about housing, or of the secretary of Agriculture to be concerned about farm income. This is the way government has been structured. Before I, as an educator, accuse such officials of venality, I must remember that those representing education as an interest group also have no difficulty looking to the secretary of HEW to push programs of benefit to them, without bothering much about the possibly better uses of those resources elsewhere.

Yet at some place in government the general-welfare point of view must be brought into focus, and that place is the presidency. The Council of Economic Advisers and its chairman will tend almost instinctively to take the general-welfare point of view both because they do not themselves have particularized constituencies and because the discipline of economics trains people to think in so-called opportunity-cost terms. Resources used here are resources that cannot be used there. The results of using them "here" must not only be good but good enough to warrant giving up what could be had from alternative uses. Students, of course, must "think economically" about the use of their time. By devoting more time to his or her favorite subject of economics, for example, a student's grade might go from B to A, which in itself is good, but it might be a bad deal if the resulting reduction of time spent on English Composition changes that student's grade from C to F.

This opportunity cost and benefit calculus is inherently the president's point of view. He must look explicitly at the "other side" of any affirmative decision about programs because all of the parts must come together and be added up there into a program for which he is responsible.

Third, the CEA chairman and his agency have primary responsibility for the administration's annual economic report. The importance of this should not be denigrated for a good reason. Articulation makes policy. The requirement that the president and the CEA lay out each year their evaluation of the economy and the implications for policy makes for more explicit thinking and therefore better policy. These reports through the years have been of uneven quality, but the CEA chairman should treat the production of these reports as a high-priority claim on time. Policies will be better for writing this report, and needed public understanding will be more effectively advanced.

Two other operational comments. First, the CEA chairman, and his boss in the Oval Office also, will search in vain for the control room containing all of those powerful levers by which a president is supposed to keep the economy on some prescribed course. While differences of opinion remain, most economists agree that monetary policy is at least important. Monetary policy, however, is the responsibility of a Federal Reserve independent of the White House and directly responsible to the Congress. While there is close consultation between the president and his associates and the Federal Reserve, the president cannot decree that monetary policy be changed. And history provides numerous episodes of presidents vexed and frustrated by a Federal Reserve that carried out its own ideas. (And history shows that the Federal Reserve was not always right.)

As for fiscal policy, major changes reflect Congressional legislation, which is a cumbersome process. When the president escalated the Vietnam War in 1966, he did not go for a needed tax increase, we are told, because he decided that the Congress would balk, though it was overwhelmingly controlled by his own party and he had been majority leader of the Senate. For many programs, outlays are literally uncontrollable—for example, social security benefits. And for some whose outlays are in the formal sense controllable, viscosities are such that changes in their rate of spending will occur slowly.

It is important to keep these limitations in mind. The fact is that we hold the president politically accountable for the results of policies over which his range of control is surprisingly restricted. Not only the president and his advisers but the rest of us need to remember this. Disillusionment may be caused by illusions of effectiveness that never had any realistic basis in fact.

Now to my final operational point. An academic economist walking into that office *de novo* will probably find himself spending a much larger proportion of his time on so-called micro-policy matters than was his original expectation. The global issues of the budget and monetary policy and inflation and output get the headlines, but the impact of government on the functioning of the economic system depends heavily on the aggregate of much more specific policies and programs. And the CEA chairman will often in these matters find himself in an embattled position against politically powerful alliances between interest groups and "their agencies" in Washington. During my own tenure, these issues ranged through such matters as agricultural prices, limitations on the number of New York City taxicabs, the adjustment of interest rate ceilings on government bonds, constrictions on coal-hauling capacity, and deregulation of trucking—just to name a few.

Nor should our emigre from academe assume that these are either easy or unimportant issues. Regulated industries may at times complain about specific regulatory decisions, but regulatory commissions and their industries are apt to be allied in opposition to decontrol. Regulation creates vested interests that really become the capitalized value of artificial shortages. Because the number of New York taxicabs has been restricted, the current value of a medallion (the right to operate a taxi) now ranges up to roughly $40,000. The result is that service is poorer and taxi fares obviously must be high enough to cover normal costs, wages, and a return on this $40,000. With deregulation, riders would have better service, rates would be lower, and drivers' earnings would be no lower and probably higher. But the industry would probably oppose deregulation because of their investment in the status quo.

If all that the Interstate Commerce Commission (ICC) had cost the U.S. economy during its long and inglorious life had been the aggregate of its annual budgets, we would be fortunate. The real cost has been a railroad industry in shambles and perhaps one-third more trucks using up fuel on the highways than is really necessary to haul the cargoes. Yet it is the ICC and the industries their regulation has so messed up that will join together in opposing deregulation.

How does an increase in the minimum wage distribute itself among an increase in the price-cost level, in unemployment, and in such other effects as reduced earnings elsewhere? If the investment tax credit were changed,what would be the effect on capital formation? What would a change in the price of oil do to our price level? What will be the impact of the auto strike on the economy? These are just a few of the myriad of questions that involve policy decisions, and where economic analysis can be helpful.

As we look at the period ahead, it seems clear that a major concern of economic policy will be to get the proportion of output going into capital formation—new and better plants and machinery—up from levels that have prevailed in the 1970s. If we do not, the rate of gain in real incomes will decline, and before the expansion has fully reemployed the labor force, we will have run short of plant capacity. But for a nail, a kingdom may be lost.

Now to some readers all of this discussion about capital formation will seem a bit arcane and esoteric. Yet impressionistically we can all see that how much a person produces depends in part on how much capital equipment backs up or reinforces human labor. In poor countries it is not unusual to see on road projects men and women carrying dirt or gravel in a basket. The amount of dirt moved per man-hour there is obviously less than in, say, Michigan, where we equip a man with an earth-moving behemoth. In the typical poor economy, the proportion of the labor force in agriculture is high, and food consumption is low. In the United States today, 3.8 percent of the labor force is in agriculture, and a well-written book on how to lose weight is almost a certain best seller. Why? A major reason for the difference is that, supplementing the physical and mental efforts of each U.S. farmer is a powerful tractor (and probably two or three of them), a combine costing perhaps $50,000, and back at the barns a piggery that rivals the farmer's comfortable and modern house in cost.

Traditionally the stock of capital per person in the labor force has increased about 2.5 percent per year. Thus far in the 1970s the figure has been about 1.6 percent. If we do not get this process back on the rails, and make up our arrearages, the economy's capability to sustain rising material levels of living and reasonably full employment will progressively weaken.

The most critical aspect of this problem is that ours has become a low-profit economy. Now a benevolent view toward profits does not characterize our society today, and that is perhaps particularly evident within academe itself. But we had better ponder some hard facts. Because of archaic accounting procedures, costs are understated and profits are overstated in an inflation. This would not be serious perhaps except that corporations incur a tax liability for roughly half of this overstatement of profits. When profits are recalculated to allow more accurately for true economic costs, we find some interesting things. "True" corporate profits after taxes in 1976, even with the rise from the recession, were equal to perhaps 3.5 percent of GNP compared with 6.5 percent for 1966. And earnings retained after dividends paid out were about $18 billion in 1976, well below the $29 billion a decade ago even though the price level in that decade rose 74 percent. Real corporate retained earnings in 1976, in short, were about one-third of those a decade earlier.

If this pattern continues, the U.S. economy will face some combination of secular unemployment and weakened gains in productivity and real incomes.

Second, economic policy in the years ahead must come to terms with a new realism about inflation. In varying degrees both here and in other major economies we have seen a congealing of views around certain points. First, there is growing skepticism about the old view that an economy can operate at sustained higher rates of growth in production and employment if only we are willing to operate at, say 6 percent unemployment rather than 4 percent. When people are "thinking 4 percent" and rates of interest are based on expectations of 4 percent, heating the economy on up to a 6 percent rate of inflation may temporarily give a spurt to output and employment. The trouble is that people learn. Interest rates then rise to a level consistent with 6 percent inflation, and expectations generally adjust. These surges, in short, can only be achieved with accelerating rates of inflation, not just with a higher but steady-state rate. And, for very good reasons, accelerating rates of inflation always end in a top-side collision, recession, and unemployment.

More broadly, there are growing doubts about whether high rates of inflation and liberal (that is, free and open), democratic institutions are compatible. Evidence about the distortions and displacement effects of inflation is in an appallingly primitive state, but the severely adverse effects of inflation on consumer sentiment (which can be measured) are at least circumstantial evidence that they are more extensive than analysis to date have identified. If these major distortions are there, and I suspect that they are, this would help to explain the rising demand during inflation for the illiberal approach of direct controls—which in turn produce shortages, further distortions, growing corruption, and finally failure.

It is easy to be pessimistic about our prospects for reducing further the rate of inflation. The arithmetic of the price level, whether produced by econometric models or by less formalized means, makes it difficult to be optimistic about our prospects for working the rate of inflation down further. The price level always tracks closely with labor costs per unit of output for the obvious reason that they are the dominant element in total costs. With compensation per man-hour rising at about a 7.5 percent per-year rate, and with the trend rate of improvement in productivity not over 2.5 percent and possibly now closer to 2 percent, the basic path for the price level would seem to be rising at 5–5.5 percent per year. A rate of inflation at, say, 3 percent per year would require getting wage adjustments down to the 5 percent zone, and it is not easy to prescribe the process by which that is to be achieved.

Yet we must remember that the ability of formal economic analysis to predict rates of inflation has been found to be severely limited. Our models did not earlier predict the degree to which the rate of inflation was destined to accelerate. Their inability to project an acceptable path for further deceleration of inflation may well reflect less the inability of the economy to regain a more stable price level than the limitations of our economic models. What we do know is that governments that have followed sustained policies more consistent with price-level stability have turned in superior economic performances.

Yet our CEA chairman and his principal must also be concerned about the fact that there are unemployed people, and society must be responsive to this problem. The first requirement is that we see the dynamics, the moving picture, of unemployment. Even when the unemployment rate does not change, a surprisingly large proportion of the people unemployed this month were not unemployed last month and will not be unemployed next month. In 1973, for example, the median duration of unemployment was less than five weeks, and even in 1976 it was about eight weeks and falling. For most of these people, the problem is to maintain income during a relatively short interruption of earnings.

There are, however, 1–2 million who represent the problem of chronic unemployment. For them the problem is not a temporary interruption of earnings, lasting a few weeks, but a persisting lack of employment. There are, of course, many reasons for this—ranging from excessive minimum-wage levels that freeze those with minimal skills and training out of jobs, to an educational system that adjusts with the speed of a glacier to changing patterns of job opportunities. Whatever the causes of their problem, we need some sort of direct public employment programs if—and this is by no means certain—these wage rates can be kept somewhat below those in the economy generally. Otherwise we would simply have set in action another engine to give us more wage-cost-price inflation.

Finally, our CEA chairman must advise his principal about the management of policies recognizing that external economic developments now have a profound effect on the performance of our domestic economy. This is something new. Two decades ago, a brief period as history goes, per capita income in the United Kingdom was about 45 percent of that here, and for Japan the figure was one-quarter of that in the United Kingdom. France was about even with the United Kingdom, and Germany was behind them both. The world economy today is a different place. Germany's per capita income is close to ours, and France is not far behind. Japan's per capita income is now close to three-quarters of ours and 25 percent higher than that of the United Kingdom. Indeed, Japan is today the second largest of the liberal economies. There is now, in short, a lot of purchasing power "out there," and it can exert an important influence on the U.S. economy. During the 1974–75 recession, for example, our own foreign trade position improved sharply. Because of this, domestic employment at the bottom of the recession was roughly one million higher than would otherwise have been the case.

While this all means many things for domestic policy, two points deserve particular emphasis. In the management of domestic economic policies, external economic policies must quite explicitly be taken into account. And there must be particularly close coordination of domestic economic policies by Germany, Japan, and the United States because these are the strong economies, and their moving along a course of reasonably stable and sustained expansion is an essential condition for world economic stability.

At the beginning of this essay, I alluded to the possibility that if King Solomon had signed the Employment Act, the writer of

Ecclesiastes would have added that there is a time for the CEA chairman to get out. By now another may have occurred to the reader— namely, that there is a time for an essay to end. And the rule for that, as it happens, is the same as for any CEA chairman's disembarkation: The right time at the time will seem to be too soon, at least for the author of the essay.

3

ECONOMIC PROBLEMS
AND ECONOMIC ADVICE:
A HALF-CENTURY
OF EVOLUTION
Roy Blough

This essay is written in response to the question posed to me, "What would I advise now?" That question, good at any time, is especially appropriate today. Consider the problems we face: a persistent inflation spiraling at higher rates than in any earlier peacetime period; a stubbornly high level of unemployment; a rate of growth of GNP below that of many other countries; unjustified inequalities of income and wealth; racial and sex discrimination; decaying cities; industrial wastes that pollute the air, the land, and the seas; nuclear wastes that threaten death and destruction for thousands of years to come.

And abroad: inflation and unemployment; in many less developed countries (LDCs), dangerous levels of international debt; a burgeoning world population; demands by the LDCs for a "New International Economic Order"; an Organization of Petroleum Exporting Countries (OPEC) cartel toward which other nations seem powerless to develop an effective unified policy. And the growing threat of nuclear terrorism, even holocaust.

It is not news, but it still seems paradoxical that a society that can achieve such great advances in technology—transportation, communication, outer space, nuclear energy, medicine—and which has a large body of trained economists armed with high-powered analytical tools and computerized data processing, has not achieved better-managed national economies, not to mention a world economy. To the radical economist, the paradox presents no intellectual problem: The capitalistic system is simply moving on its ineluctable way toward its foreordained collapse. Believe that if you wish. But while the capitalistic system has undergone substantial evolution and like its prececessors no doubt will eventually evolve into something substantially different, plans for an early funeral are in my view highly premature. And, certainly, to choose deliberately to shift to some other system, which, if it has been used at all, has no record of success at all comparable to that of our own, strikes me as lacking in rationality. It certainly does not appeal to me. The sensible course is to improve what we have; that has been the purpose of economic policy.

Economic policy has largely to do with measures taken by the political government to influence the activities of private economic units. A perfect working of Adam Smith's "unseen hand" would make such measures unnecessary. But long and sad experience has demonstrated that self-interest frequently does not coincide with the public interest. When this occurs, governmental intervention is undertaken to help preserve the values of private enterprise while promoting the public purposes of efficient production and broad and equitable distribution. This is easier said than done, and in case it proves to be impossible, it may be necessary to suppress the private activity or to supplement private activity with government activity. These should be the last resort, not the first choice. The rule should be: that government is best which governs least, while achieving public values in optimum degree. A fact that adds difficulty is that economic freedom of action is itself one of our important public values to be weighed against other values that can be achieved only by restraining economic freedom.

Whatever agreement there may be with this rule—and I think that as long as we stick to generalities there may be a good deal of agreement—there clearly are wide differences of opinion, even among economists, regarding economic policy. Such disagreements can arise from many sources: the models accepted as showing how the economy works under simplifying assumptions; beliefs regarding the impact of social and political institutions on economic behavior; priorities among public values such as liberty, order, efficiency, equality, and so on; not to mention simple self-interest, which may be the most important of all. More specifically, with respect to the approaches to economic policy that I shall be considering, are differences of opinion on (1) the effectiveness and speed of action of automatic self-correcting forces in the private economy, (2) the patience of the public in waiting for the self-correcting forces to work, (3) the effectiveness of public action on the operations of the economy, and (4) which is to be trusted the more, the economic process or the political process. There obviously is room for major differences of judgment on each of these points among sincere and intelligent people.

I return, as I shall from time to time, to the question "What would I advise now?" At this point the emphasis is on the *now*. The "now" of economic advice is an important consideration. Some economists—and I am not pointing at members of the Council of Economic Advisers—have given the same economic policy advice decade after decade. I am suspicious of advice that never changes. The need for changes in the application of policy measures to meet changes in the stage of the business cycle is clear, although the public finds difficulty in understanding even shifts of this character. But I am thinking mainly of longer-term or secular changes. There are few if any absolutes or universals in economics. Man's behavior in a social setting is affected by such factors as the numbers and location of population, the economic structures and distribution of economic power, political and social institutions, public attitudes, and the degree of international interdependence. All of these vary from place to place and change over time. Economic policy is not forever; it must fit the time and place.

To examine the relationship between changes in the economy, improvements in our tools for understanding the economy and influencing its behavior, and the economic advice that should be given, I have chosen the period of the past half-century. Fifty years is long enough to discern major trends, and short enough to be encompassed frequently in the professional lifetime of a single observer. The years I shall concentrate on are 1926, my starting point; 1946, when the Employment Act was passed, officially introducing fiscal policy; 1951, when the Federal Reserve became freer to use monetary policy; and 1976, the present. I cannot deny that there is a personal factor attracting me to the selection of these years. In 1926 I was about to enter upon my first nonacademic job as a professional economist, with the Wisconsin State Tax Commission. In 1946 I left the U.S. Treasury Department and started teaching taxation and fiscal policy at the University of Chicago. In 1951 I was a member of President Harry Truman's Council of Economic Advisers and its liaison member on tax and monetary policy with the treasury and the Federal Reserve. This means that I shall be drawing on my memory; accordingly, this essay may be deemed to reflect a pattern of accumulated personal biases. But of whose words may this not be said?

The first step here is to relate changes in the economy, changes in the understanding of the economy, and changes in the dominant economic policy advice between 1926 and the passage of the Employment Act of 1946. The goals of the Employment Act—to promote "maximum production, employment, and purchasing power"—were not new in 1946; they are implicit in all of economics and undoubtedly have been present throughout human history. What was new and significant in 1946 was the formal acceptance by the federal government of responsibility for promoting the achievement of these goals.

Government intervention in the U.S. economy is nothing new. It was well established by 1926. Indeed, such intervention dates from the earliest days of the republic. The first law passed by Congress in 1789 imposed an import duty for the stated dual purpose of raising revenue and protecting U.S. industry. Government provided the early economy with physical infrastructure in the form of highways and canals. Building of the transcontinental railways was subsidized by enormous grants of land. The Homestead Act of 1862 made free land available to settlers who would develop it. A little later, the federal government began to regulate certain business activities. Industries deemed to be natural monopolies were regulated as to prices and services. The Sherman Antitrust Act and the Clayton Act were passed in an effort to restore and maintain competition, which had been undermined by the formation of trusts. The Federal Trade Commission Act was passed to prohibit, as unfair, the types of competition that were leading to monopoly. The Federal Reserve System was established to provide a potential pool of credit for the nation's banks to draw on as a defense against financial panic. Laws had been passed to protect workers and consumers from unsafe factories, dangerous drugs, impure foods, and so on. There were even the beginnings of a conservation movement, although the early laws applied only to government-owned land.

Despite these forms of governmental intervention, however, one of the most firmly held beliefs of businessmen and of the mainstream of economists a half century ago was that, as far as the central structure of the economy was concerned, government intervention could only be harmful. It was believed that the economic system had an inbuilt tendency to use all its resources and to allocate them where they would produce the greatest personal and social advantage. Furthermore, the system was believed to be automatically self-correcting. If the equilibrium of the economy were disturbed by the injection of some extraneous factor, compensatory forces within the economy would operate to move it back toward full-employment equilibrium. J. B. Seay's early nineteenth-century law of markets—roughly speaking, that supply creates its own demand so that general overproduction is impossible—was a central tenet of the faith. Underlying this system of belief were the assumptions that resources moved quickly within the economy under the stimulus of relative price changes and that returns to the factors of production, notably wages and interest, would rise and fall to equalize the supply and demand of the factors in the market.

To be sure, there had been from time to time financial panics and periods of severe unemployment and disequilibrium; these were deemed to be unusual and temporary and an inevitable cost of a system well worth that cost. This euphoric view of the economic system was standard doctrine in 1926, although there were of course Marxists and other dissenters, as well as a few economists who were studying the effects of legal and other institutions on the norms of economic behavior. But in 1926, believers in the "true faith" seemed to have little cause for misgivings. It was, as I recall it, a time of optimism and of complacency regarding economic policies, at least in governmental circles. The Republican party was firmly entrenched in power. The slogan "back to normalcy" had won in the election of 1920, and that of "hands off business" in the election of 1924. The dominant influence and moral authority of business were only weakly challenged, if at all, in the executive, legislative, and judicial branches of the federal government. The economy appeared to be in good shape, with rising levels of production, relatively stable prices, and an improbably low recorded rate of unemployment of 1 percent of the labor force. The balance of international payments was satisfactory. To be sure, there were problems in some sectors of the economy. Agricultural surpluses and low prices were proving to be recalcitrant. The Florida land boom and collapse indicated an excess of euphoria and speculative psychology. But in general the experience of the economy was demonstrating the rightness of the traditional doctrines. The proper role of government, obviously, was to balance the budget annually, to pay off national debt that might have been incurred for war or other purposes, to assure the supply of money and credit needed by business, but to keep its hands off of business and the economy generally.

The extent to which this imposing economic and political edifice rested on weak, even rotten foundations was soon revealed by the financial crisis of 1929 and the slide into deep depression over the next three years. Traditional economists waited for the compensating, self-correcting forces to turn the economy around. Other people became tired of waiting and increasingly insisted on action. The Democrats with Franklin Roosevelt at the head of the ticket were elected in 1932.

The remarkable series of laws passed in the early New Deal years, many during the first 100 days, reassured the public that finally something was being done. The new laws were designed to achieve several purposes: to provide relief from suffering, to protect hard-pressed debtors, to stop the downward slide, and to correct serious flaws in economic institutions, notably security markets, holding companies, banks, and labor-management relations. The price of gold was increased 70 percent. The laws by and large were successful in bringing the decline to an end and in laying the foundations for a sounder economy, but the expected expansionary response from business was not forthcoming. There was some recovery, but despite a growing labor force, GNP continued below 1929 levels.

Meanwhile other measures were being proposed. A number of "intellectuals" or "pseudo-intellectuals" some of them of my acquaintance, made a sort of living lecturing on their favorite nostrums. Pump-priming was a popular idea; it was based on the analogy of the farmer's pump whose valve leathers had become dry. Only a little "water"—that is, government spending—it was argued, would be needed to put the pump back to normal. Government spending did indeed increase, but without substantially improving the functioning of the economic pump. Many proposals concentrated on methods of stimulating private spending. A favorite proposal was to encourage rapid monetary turnover by issuing currency to which a stamp would have to be affixed every 30 days by the unfortunate holder on that date. A stated purpose of the undistributed profits tax of 1936, which the administration proposed and Congress passed in somewhat emasculated form, was to move money out of the coffers of business, where it was not being spent, into the hands of stockholders, who being also consumers, presumably would spend it. In 1938 the law was repealed, with few mourners at its grave.

Curiously enough, proposals for large increases in government spending for the purpose of enlarging the total spending stream were long rejected out of hand. At one point Senator Robert La Follette of Wisconsin proposed a $10 billion spending program, but it was deemed inflationary and socialistic and was never taken seriously. Roosevelt had been elected in 1932 on a platform of drastic budget cutting and a balanced budget. Throughout the early 1930s, indeed through 1937, an administration goal continued to be to balance the budget; to that end measures designed to increase tax revenues were passed in every year, 1932 through 1937. In November 1937, Secretary of the Treasury Henry Morgenthau proudly announced in a public address that the federal budget had been balanced in the previous month. The fact that this statement was greeted by derisive and unseemly laughter by his business audience might have warned him; at any rate, the economy was already moving downward into a recession within the depression.

The esteem in which business was held took a great fall between 1926 and 1936, a fall that the administration did nothing to soften, to say the least. The decline in esteem was no doubt due in part simply to the fact that things were going badly and unemployment was very high. It was due in part to the discovery by congressional committess of a great amount of skullduggery by many financiers and other businessmen during the 1920s, which cost hundreds of thousands of investors huge sums of money. In part, however, the decline in the esteem toward business was due to continued faith in the traditional economic beliefs. It was obvious that something was desperately wrong. The inference was not so much that economic policy was wrongly conceived as that the businessmen had been "bad boys" and were not carrying out their responsibilities. This "bad boy" concept of business embittered relations between the government and the business community.

Government expenditures started to increase almost immediately after Roosevelt's inauguration in 1933. However, these increases were not deliberately designed to restore prosperity but rather were found necessary to prevent widespread starvation and public disorder—hence the Federal Emergency Relief Administration, the Works Progress Administration, and the Public Works Administration. Dr. Francis E. Townsend's movement for a $200 per month payment to all elderly people was excoriated and defeated but undoubtedly was influential in the decision to pass the Social Security Act and other welfare legislation. Indeed, it should be noted and emphasized that the new addition to forms of federal government intervention in the economy during the 1930s was not deficit spending but the embryo of the welfare state, the maturing of which was postponed until the 1960s and 1970s.

It was only in 1938 that the president, persuaded both by the dismal history of the previous years and by advisers who had been "infected" with the new Keynesian theories, gave up the effort to achieve a balanced budget and turned to expenditure increases despite the deficits. The long delay in turning to deficit spending as a method of dealing with the depression was partly because of the fear that to do so would undermine the confidence of businessmen, investors, and other private spenders to such an extent that a net decrease in total spending would result. The delay was due also to the fact that prior to the publication in 1936 of John Maynard Keynes's famous work, *The General Theory of Employment, Money, and Interest*, proponents of deficit spending were generally considered to be "crackpots." Keynes gave scholarly credibility to proposals that were by no means new but were not considered respectable. The shift to deficit spending was made easier by the growing recognition of the approaching war in Europe and the sad state of U.S. preparedness for war. The acceptance of vast federal outlays and deficit spending in times of war has been as much a part of American tradition as were annually balanced budgets and minimum spending for social programs in times of peace. With the preparation for war and entry into it, the depression evaporated, and the problem shifted from underemployment and insufficient demand to over-full employment and excessive demand. Under administration prodding, taxes were increased repeatedly until Congress and the public balked and refused to do more. The tax revenues collected during the war covered only about half of the expenditures. War taxes were accompanied in suppressing inflation by rationing and price controls, and perhaps even more importantly by the nonproduction of automobiles, appliances, and many other items.

During the war, several nuclei of economists, mostly of the Keynesian persuasion, were set up in the new war agencies and elsewhere. New statistical tools, such as the GNP and input-output analysis, were becoming available. The "inflationary gap" was analyzed in the framework of a national economic budget. A missionary campaign to win converts to Keynesian principles among economists already in the government had considerable success, being made easier by the fact that Keynesian policy toward war finance closely resembles traditional policy.

Throughout the war, there was a widely shared fear both in the United States and in other countries that when the war ended the economy would drop back into depression. A good deal of "postwar planning" went on, and out of this grew the Full Employment Bill of 1945, which in greatly modified form was passed as the Employment Act of 1946. It should not be assumed that everyone had become a convert to Keynesian principles. However, many high-level civil servants, some key administration political figures, and a relatively few members of Congress were at least prepared to try them. But there was also vigorous opposition from those who opposed government intervention as a matter of principle, and those who feared that government promises, and what would be involved in their implementation, would open a Pandora's box.

The Full Employment Bill of 1945 contained in its declaration of policy a truly revolutionary pronouncement as far as the U.S. government was concerned—namely, "All Americans able to work and seeking work have the right to useful, remunerative, regular, and full-time employment. . . ." The proposed implementation of this proposed right was directly out of Keynes as interpreted by his American disciples. The administration was to develop and propose to Congress a "national budget of production and employment," which was to include an estimate of the demand necessary to keep and maintain full employment. Estimates were to be made also of how much demand the private economy could be expected to contribute. The government was then to provide sufficient additional expenditure and investment to assure realization of the total demand needed for full employment. There was more in the bill, but this was the essence. There was no provision for a Council of Economic Advisers.

The 1945 bill, with some changes, passed the Senate, but the House was more conservative. Members objected that the bill promised a great deal too much. They did not like promising employment to everyone who wanted employment. They did not like the term "full employment," arguing that it was impossible to define. They did not want a national production and employment budget with a presumption that government expenditures and investment would make up any shortages in private expenditures and investment. However, the pressure to pass an employment act was overwhelming. The Employment Act of 1946 was a compromise. Its declaration of policy calls for the government to draw on almost every method imaginable to promote "maximum production, employment, and purchasing power." But the act does not promise anything; it establishes no rights. It accepts for the federal government the responsibility to promote conditions for achieving maximum production, employment, and purchasing power. This was a very important step, but not a promise of employment. More or less as an afterthought to give substance to the act, it provided for a Council of Economic Advisers to the president to help him prepare an economic report to the Congress. The council was to be made up of qualified persons of equal rank, except that one was to be designated chairman. The act also established a joint committee in the Congress to receive the economic report of the president and to react to it. That, in short, was the act passed in 1946.

A person reading the Employment Act would notice certain inconsistencies that clearly indicated two philosophies struggling and ending in a compromise. For example, the federal government was "to coordinate and utilize all its plans, functions, and resources" to achieve the purposes of the act, and to do this "in a manner calculated to foster and promote free competitive enterprise." Planning and free competitive enterprise seem poles apart, but as I shall discuss later, I consider their combination in certain sectors to be in practice needed for the successful management of prosperity.

However, we should not leave the Employment Act without noticing what it does not contain, since this will indicate areas not deemed to be the special concern of the council. There is no mention of inflation, although the law was debated and passed in a period of both repressed and open inflation. "Maximum purchasing power" has been of necessity interpreted to relate to price stability, since employment policy without concern for inflation would be unthinkable, or at least unthinking. There was no mention of the balance of payments, or of international equilibrium. Surprisingly, there was no mention of economic or social justice, or of the distribution of income or wealth, let alone their redistribution. Moreover, fighting words used toward business in the 1930s are completely absent. Their omission was scarcely accidental. To omit them was politically very wise, and it was possible because it reflected the new national unity that the war had achieved. But it also reflected a basic shift in economic understanding. Depressions, it now appeared, were not caused by "bad boys of business"; the problem was more fundamental. Private business enterprise could be expected to develop fluctuations and other deficiencies that required compensatory action by government if they were to be corrected without intolerable delay.

This did not mean that the old tools of policy were of no further use. Some of them, such as antitrust policy, were recognized as being of increasing importance. Nor did it mean that everyone would accept the new approach. Quite the contrary; the controversy continues to this day.

The Employment Act grew out of the fear of renewed depression and was directed to the problem of unemployment. But I think the real concern of the country was for the much broader subject of the role of the federal government in the economy generally—what various writers have called the management of prosperity. The very first Economic Report of the president and that of the council,* issued in January 1947, said little about employment and much about inflation as well as many other matters. It incorporated the president's whole economic program, domestic and foreign. Even the embryo of the wage-price guidelines was there: "For its own advantage as well as that of the country at large, labor should refrain from demands for excessive wage increases that would require price increases." Subsequent reports of the president, as well as the reports of the council, continued to cover a broad scope.

Thus, even before the first Economic Report, the immediate concern had moved from unemployment to inflation. The combined economic objective had become high employment with price stability. Before long, economic expansion and growth also became an objective of governmental policy. The second chairman of the council, Leon Keyserling, in particular, took the initiative in the early promotion of this objective, linking it to both employment and national strength. The combined objective thus before many years became economic growth at high employment with price stability. This three-legged objective was generally accepted, but which of the legs is the most important was and continues to be widely debated. There are, of course, other policy objectives involving conflicts of interest over distribution of income, but the universally accepted ones that mark a viable economy are economic growth, low unemployment, and stable prices.

---

*The original Truman Council included Edwin G. Nourse, chairman; Leon H. Keyserling, vice-chairman; and John D. Clark. They took the oath of office August 9, 1946. Nourse left the council November 1, 1949. Keyserling became chairman and Clark became vice-chairman May 10, 1950. Roy Blough took the oath of office June 29, 1950 and left the council August 20, 1952. Robert C. Turner took the oath of office September 8, 1952 and left office January 20, 1953; Keyserling left on that date and Clark left as of February 11, 1953.

My concern here with the Truman council is with its economic advice, and I must pass over its pioneering contributions in organization, procedures, and analytical and expository devices. Since the council was made up of persons with differing philosophies, the advice was not always unanimously agreed to, but the following will perhaps serve as a summary.

Fiscal policy. Until mid-1949, the council recommended a budget surplus, to be achieved through either maintaining taxes or increasing them to fight inflation. Expenditure reduction also was recommended in these early postwar years. The council worked strongly for higher taxes to finance the Korean War.

Monetary policy. Credit restraints were supported, including both general restraints achieved through increasing bank reserve requirements and also restraints on consumer credit, and during the Korean War, on housing credit. The council at no time recommended abandoning the Federal Reserve support at par value of long-term low-interest government bonds, and when the accord between the Treasury and the Federal Reserve in early 1951 permitted the abandonment of such support, Clark publicly opposed doing this, even after President Truman accepted it.

Wages and prices. The danger of the inflationary spiral was frequently reiterated and the folly of pushing up wages and prices was stressed. The council was divided on the desirability of reimposing price controls in the fall of 1950, but supported the price freeze when it came early in 1951. Stand-by powers to impose wage and price controls had been urged previously.

Priorities and allocations. The experience of World War II showed the importance of shortages and bottlenecks as a cause of inflation. With some differences of opinion, the council recommended that the power to determine priorities and make allocations be held by the president and exercised when needed for balanced growth.

Planning. Certain members of the council as well as members of the staff were active in drafting and promoting the Spence and Murray bills of 1949, both of which had a large role for national planning. Nourse reported that he refused to sign a proposed council review, which would have recommended various features of these bills.[1]

There were various other aspects to the advice of the council, but I believe these were the most important. Reference has been made to differences of opinion among council members. To a minor degree, this was reflected in different assessments of the move from inflation to disinflation in 1949. But much more important were the differences in basic philosophy. A good statement of these appears in the Tenth Anniversary Symposium sponsored by the National Planning

Association.[2] Edwin G. Nourse, the first chairman of the council, differentiated between those persons who looked for the act to "launch the Federal Government on a comprehensive and continuous program for engineering optimum performance for the whole economy" and "those who understood the Act as merely stating a broad objective or ideal goal toward which effort would be directed and as introducing additions to our executive and legislative institutions which would aid the economy—both its private and its public sectors—in moving more competently toward that goal." Nourse placed himself in the latter group. The vice-chairman and second council chairman, Leon H. Keyserling, was firmly in the optimum performance group. He called for presidential leadership and initiative, noting that "the commitment of the Employment Act to full-employment economics rather than to countercyclical economics . . . represents a profoundly valuable and virile shift in mood and emphasis." There were also differences in the attitude toward giving economic advice to the Congress. This is not provided in the act, but the congressional committees continually pressed the council to tell them what the President had been advised or at least to give them advice also. Nourse did not consider this to be appropriate; Keyserling stated that he saw no problem in advising the Congress in the same fashion as the President.

These problems were accentuated by the structure of the council. All three members were equal, with the same rights and authority, except that one was designated chairman. In many three-man groups this causes problems in getting work done, but this was not a problem in the council. There was, however, the problem of "speaking with one mind" when the members were not of one mind. There was also the problem of representation. It was not practical for all three members of the council to be present at meetings when other agencies each had only one representative. Usually it was possible to designate the chairman or another member as representative, but on really important matters, each member wanted to be able to defend his own position. As a result there were various meetings held at which the council should have been represented but to which it was not invited because of the representation problem.

The council had some of the problems that might be expected whenever a new group comes into the system closer to the top than those already functioning. Certain agencies with particular programs to administer flatly refused to modify the timing of their operations to help stabilize the economy, on the grounds that their responsibility was to administer matters entrusted to them by Congress, and they did not feel bound by anything as general as the Employment Act.

In its early years the Council of Economic Advisers was near the center of Washington attention. However, with the start of the Korean War and its continuation, new war agencies were established and the influence over policy, as well as public interest, gradually shifted over to them. Moreover, hostility in Congress, which had always been present, seemed to be growing. There had been difficulties on more than one occasion with appropriation subcommittees. In the summer of 1952, about the time I was leaving the council to go to the United Nations, the appropriations subcommittee of the House cut the council's budget by 25 percent. Some defenders of the council conceived the idea of having the appropriation spent over only nine months, thereby leaving the council staff intact for that period, but with no funds after March 31, 1953. It was assumed that whichever party won the election would pass a supplementary appropriation. However, there was no move from the new administration to secure such an appropriation. For all practical purposes, the council went out of business when its money ran out at the end of March 1953. Arthur F. Burns was sworn in as chairman on March 19. While there was some sentiment for letting the council die, or substituting a single councilor, the law was revised (through a presidential reorganization plan) to make the chairman in effect the council, but with other members whom he would presumably choose. The council was restored to life with an entirely new professional staff, with one or two exceptions, and was run with a new philosophy.

The council after the Truman Administration is represented by other writers in this volume. During the Eisenhower years, 1953–61, both the party in power and the economic philosophy were different from what had gone on before and what came afterward. The first Eisenhower chairman, Arthur F. Burns, in a communication to the Tenth Anniversary Symposium previously referred to, indicated agreement with those who believed that "the government could probably help in some degree to moderate economic fluctuations without intruding unduly into private affairs or becoming a dominant factor in our economy." By the time a more positive role for government was undertaken in the Kennedy administration, the experience of the Truman council probably was viewed pretty much as past and not very relevant history.

The congressional Joint Economic Committee and its staff played an important role in the operation of the Employment Act. It was well situated, despite its lack of bill-reporting powers, because it had forward-looking chairmen and committee members during most years, an able and imaginative staff, money, and no immediate administrative or legislative responsibilities. The hearings and symposiums of the joint committee and its subcommittee gave the academic community a much-appreciated sounding board for advanced ideas. The committee could continue a positive approach despite the change in administration. The staff made projections of potential economic growth and showed the failure of the economy to achieve its potential. In many areas of policy the committee laid the foundations for later adoption of more effective tools of analysis, and it served an educational function, making the Congress better prepared to accept a more activist economic policy.

A modern Rip van Winkle who fell asleep in 1950 and awoke in 1975 might not notice much difference in his immediate physical surroundings but would soon discover that major economic and social changes had taken place, both domestically and internationally. For comment here, I have selected six developments that have major significance for the policies needed to promote the goals of the Employment Act.

1. *The growing power of private collective action.* It was already recognized a quarter-century ago that large business organizations and labor organizations were able to raise their prices and wages even in the presence of falling demand simply because of the economic power of numbers of people and numbers of dollars working collectively. The rising prices and wages are passed on to buyers where possible. Moreover, the increases spread through imitation into unrelated industries, since business and labor leaders believe that to keep their jobs as well as their self-esteem they must not be outdone. These tendencies have almost certainly increased in critical industries over recent decades. An added concern is that municipal employees have successfully disregarded laws against strikes in governmental services and have shown they can throttle a city by work stoppages, adding this economic power to their already considerable political power. Thus, the price of government goes up with little regard to the merits of the increases or the ability of the city to maintain its tax base in the face of higher taxes.

2. *Automation.* Some 15 or 20 years ago a great deal was being said and written to the effect that automation would make possible the production of all desired goods with a fraction of the labor force so that some method of paying people for not working would be required. Economic desires are not as easily satisfied as these prophets anticipated, and the rising real cost of fuel and minerals along with the costs of reducing pollution and restoring the environment have largely quieted the fear (or hope) of a prosperous but largely workless economy. However, unlike many earlier technological advances, automation has been reducing the job opportunities for the unskilled while creating job opportunities requiring entirely new types of skills. It is accordingly

more difficult than in earlier decades to avoid simultaneous labor surpluses and labor shortages.

3. *Rising expectations*. The belief that tomorrow would be better than today and that one's children would live better than one has lived has been a mark of American society from the beginning. There seems to have been a quantum jump in expectations since World War II. The idea that ours is an affluent society has led masses of people to believe that there is more income to be had and that they are entitled to it. But with a relatively slow rate of growth and rising costs of energy and materials and at a time when a large fraction of the product goes into military expenditures and other destinations that give no measurable benefit in consumer goods, expectations have outrun production. Given the power of collective action to force a rise in money incomes, along with a growing egalitarian movement by lower-income groups and a stubborn resistance by higher-income groups against giving up either income or position, the seeds of inflation are social as well as economic. The money illusion, which misleads different economic groups to try to get what they cannot have, has unfortunately proved to be held to very stubbornly.

4. *International pressures from less developed countries*. The revolution of rising expectations in less developed countries has also complicated the management of the U.S. economy. In 1926, U.S. policy makers did not pay much attention to the less developed countries, which were for the most part under the control of the industrially advanced countries, some as colonies or dominions, others politically independent but economically largely dependent on the industrial countries. By 1951, there were strong stirrings in the less developed countries. India had secured its independence. The United Nations had a major council devoted to seeing that dependent territories had the opportunity to become independent if they desired it. In 1953 the United Nations passed a resolution to the effect that the less developed countries retained inalienable rights over their natural resources notwithstanding any contract or treaty to the contrary.

This was only the beginning of the breakup of traditional international law as far as the less developed countries were concerned. The demands of these countries have gown with each passing year. We now have not only the OPEC petroleum cartel and efforts to imitate it for other raw materials but also a full-blown plan for a "New International Economic Order." This proposal contains virtually every imaginable change in the structure of markets, patterns of trade and investment, transfer of technology, shipping, insurance, foreign aid, and so on, that would be beneficial to the less developed countries at the expense, at least in the short run, of the industrially advanced countries. The United

32   ECONOMIC ADVICE AND EXECUTIVE POLICY

States is in a quandary. As the country with the first successful revolution in modern times, and a self-styled model for other countries, it ill-behooves the United States to reject the demands out of hand, but if it accepts them the result will require a considerable restructuring of American national production and trade.

5. *International interdependence.* U.S. relations with the industrially advanced countries also affect U.S. ability to manage its own economy. International interdependence has greatly increased over the past 25 years with the expansion of international trade and investment. U.S. import and export prices and eventually domestic prices as well are greatly affected by the shifting rates of foreign exchange. The United States cannot, except through gifts, stimulate the purchases of its goods by other countries without increasing its imports, which may cause unemployment in some U.S. industries. If the policies of other countries impair their ability to purchase U.S. goods, U.S. employment goes down. The United States is affected by their economic and trade policies and by the timing and intensity of their business cycles.

6. *Multinational corporations (MNCs).* The enormous proliferation and growth of MNCs, U.S.-based and foreign-based, has created at least potential difficulties for U.S. economic policy. It is possible, but I think not yet demonstrated, that the foreign investments of these corporations reduce U.S. employment, or, to the contrary, that their effect is to increase U.S. employment. What is certain is that since they have pro-duction facilities, research and development organizations, distribution networks, and cash balances in many countries, MNCs are in a position to shift production and accordingly employment from one country to another and to move billions of dollars of funds from one currency to another. They can thus undermine or reinforce the economic policies of national governments.

To a degree unknown before the immediate past, economic policy has to cope with a simultaneous condition of high unemployment, high inflation, and low economic growth. This calls nor recognition that there is in the economy of the 1970s more than one type of unemployment, more than one type of inflation, and more than one type of economic growth, and that the different types do not necessarily respond to the same corrective measures.

One type of economic growth is that which takes place during eco-nomic recovery when the rate of plant utilization rises from very low up toward the optimum level. Such growth can be quickly achieved as demand increases, since no new plant construction is involved. Unit costs fall, and there is no excuse for prices to be increased, assuming no increase in the cost of inputs—and indeed prices should decline, although they rarely do. When the rate of utilization is pushed by demand above the optimal level, however, unit costs rise, leading to price increases.

The other form of economic growth involves the expansion of the physical plant, assuming the availability of additional raw materials and a labor force of adequate size and having the proper mix of skills. This form of growth cannot be expected to occur unless business managers believe the demand will be forthcoming to utilize the additional capacity. If the volume of plant additions is sufficiently well timed (and assuming the prices of inputs have not risen), this kind of growth could go on indefinitely without any necessary increase in unit costs or output prices. The effects of new plants on employment and on productivity depend on the extent of technological improvement. Adding a new plant of the same design as the old one increases the potential for employment but may not result in any increase in product per man-hour. Replacing an old plant with an automated plant will increase productivity but may reduce total employment. A rise in real income depends on increased productivity, but having a job comes first.

Inflation is the increase in all prices or in some prices not offset by decreases in others. It may develop from a number of different causes. "Demand inflation" develops when general demand increases more rapidly than supply. Demand inflation ought not to develop during a recovery period when the form of growth is that of increased utilization of existing plant. However, in case of a rapid increase in expenditures when the employment of resources is at or near full (that is, optimum) utilization of critical raw materials, plant, or special labor skills, the term "bottleneck and shortage inflation" may be more accurate than general demand inflation. The expenditure increase triggering such an inflation could be in either the private or public sector, although sudden, large expenditure increases are more likely to occur in the public sector, notably in time of war. Since inflation in the bottleneck areas spreads to other areas, increased taxes and decreased government expenditures may lead to unemployment in some industries, while excess demand and inflation continue to be present in others. The sectors are out of balance, and the shift of resources is not sufficiently rapid to bring them back into balance.

"Cost-push inflation" is also a major type. Just as increased productivity—that is, decreased real costs of production—are a major restraint on inflation, so increased real costs of production force higher prices. A particular illustration is the sudden, enormous increase in petroleum prices by the OPEC countries in 1973 and other increases since that time. The real cost of production in OPEC countries had not increased and for most of these countries was far below existing prices, but for the United States the real cost did rise. The outflow of funds was not quickly matched by increased demands for our exports or by foreign investment in the United States for the production of goods and services, and accordingly the money supply of the country, held by its residents, was adversely affected. This deflationary effect presumably can be met by monetary policy, although not necessarily by general monetary increases, since some markets may be more affected than others. However, to seek to offset higher costs of petroleum in the United States by increasing wage rates would be purely inflationary since no increased productivity or restoration of lost productivity would accompany the higher wages.

"Cost-push" is also the major factor in the inflationary spiral, which tends to develop whatever the original cause of inflation. The inflationary spiral is what the United States is now suffering from, and it is the most dangerous type of inflation. The reason is that it persists because of what appears to be entirely normal and proper behavior on the part of businesses, professions, and workers. All economic units are both buyers and sellers in the circular flow of goods, services, and money through the economy. When unit costs increase for the buyer, whether of labor or of goods, it is the buyer's strong desire to increase his own selling price in order to "catch up." This seems to him and to others to be a matter of simple justice. To some extent, it is necessary if production is to continue. The higher prices are higher costs for others and are again passed on. And so on, ad infinitum.

Refusal of monetary authorities to "validate" price and wage increases, by not facilitating growth in the money supply, might restrain the increases, but are more likely to reduce employment. In the inflationary spiral, there may be no increase in real income; indeed, real income may be falling, yet the price increases go on. It is not only the pass-through of costs that contributes to the spiral. Wage increases in one industry make it politically necessary for labor leaders in other industries to match or outstrip the first increase. Business executives feel similar psychological or organizational pressures to raise their prices when others are raised.

To bring the spiral to an end, the sellers must not pass through all their cost increases, plus profit margin, in higher prices to the buyer. This is already the situation forced on millions of persons with fixed incomes, who are worst hit by the inflation. For others, the desired result might be accomplished in one of two ways. First, the seller could accept a reduction in his net real income per unit of product or hour of work. If each seller accepts less real income, the amount of money income received through higher prices will be reduced toward the available real income, and the inflationary spiral will be reduced or gradually ended. More realistic from the viewpoint of psychology would be to dedicate increases in productivity to reduce the increases in selling prices. In this case, there is no necessary decrease in anyone's real income, but the effort to secure an increase in real income is postponed until the spiral has been conquered.

When we look at what is happening to price movements and wage settlements, it is obvious that, if anything, they point to a quickening of the inflationary spiral instead of to its slowing down.

Unemployment also is of several types. First, there is frictional unemployment, the adjustments that take place in any dynamic economy, which result in shifting persons from one job to another. Frictional unemployment is commonly of relatively short duration and is the kind of unemployment that the self-adjusting mechanisms of the economy can be expected to solve without governmental intervention.

Second, there is the kind of unemployment that was so disastrous in the depression of the 1930s, namely, unemployment due to inadequate general demand. This is the kind of unemployment that fiscal policy and monetary policy were designed to overcome, and, as far as I have observed, they have been reasonably successful in doing so.

Third is the kind of unemployment that on its face looks like unemployment caused by inadequate general demand but is in fact unemployment resulting from excessive cost increases, whether in the form of wages or of material prices, in key sectors of the economy. Take wages, for example. Either the employer cannot afford to pay the highr wages, in which case he lays off workers and reduces his operations, or he shifts to labor-saving technologies, resulting in unemployment, or he succeeds in increasing his prices, thus absorbing monetary demand that otherwise would have gone for other goods and services, thereby causing unemployment in those industries. When this unemployment occurs, there is immediate pressure brought to bear on the Federal Reserve to ease monetary policy and on the administration and the Congress to reduce taxes or increase public expenditures. Thus far, these political pressures have at least in recent years always won out, with the result that the inflation has been "validated."

A fourth type of unemployment is structural unemployment. In a fully balanced economy with supply always rising to match demand and in which there are no shortages or bottlenecks, there should be no occasion for structural unemployment to occur. But, in fact, economic growth, even during a recovery, is never fully balanced. As it continues, a point is always reached where shortages and bottlenecks occur either in materials, in physical plant, or in the types of labor skills required. These bottlenecks and shortages may put a stop to growth, leaving substantial unemployment; or the costs of the elements in short supply may be increased, thus starting an inflation and possibly moving on into an inflationary spiral. Fiscal and monetary policy is effective in reducing unemployment up to the point where shortages and bottlenecks occur, but less so beyond it, some of the increased demand going into price increases. It has traditionally been assumed that the private sector will foresee demand growth and provide the necessary supply, but this obviously has not occurred on numerous occasions. Accordingly, fiscal and monetary policy cannot, at least not without substantial inflation, bring about high employment (low unemployment) in the absence of a well balanced economy. If the demand is sufficiently great, as in World War II, jobs are restructured, substitutes are found, supplies are rationed, and special governmental programs are undertaken to remove the shortages. The cost of these extraordinary measures both in inflation and in depriving consumers of their normal supplies of goods would be too great to be accepted in any situation short of major war.

Finally, a good deal of unemployment must be designated as voluntary, although technically when it is identified as being voluntary it is not counted as unemployment. But jobs are turned down every day because the job seeker considers the wage too low or the task too menial. With the welfare state in a fairly advanced stage, people can usually keep body and soul together without working, and for some there is the life of crime.

In light of the preceding interpretation of the history of the past half-century and of the present situation, what would I advise now?

Since the president might accept the council's recommendations, advice should not be given lightly. The fact that some form of intervention, or nonintervention, appears to be needed is not sufficient basis for a recommendation, since the obstacles to its achievement, the political price that may have to be paid, and the possibility of undesirable side effects must all be considered. In my ignorance of some of these matters, I shall stop short of firm recommendations for any specific measure. I shall indicate for a limited number of general policy instruments what I think is needed and why, along with a quick look at the obstacles and possible side effects involved in achieving the objective. I shall omit very short-run forecasts, leaving them to professional forecasters who have comprehensive economic models and computers at their disposal. I shall also omit commenting on very long-run problems, which I leave to the futurists. Theirs is a specialty calling for qualities of imagination that I do not have or at least do not care to exercise. One long-run assumption I do make is that there will be no major war or nuclear holocaust; without that assumption no peacetime economic policy is relevant.

Finally, I shall limit my observations to the objectives of low unemployment, stable prices, and economic growth, treating other objectives as part of the environment or frame of reference within which these objectives must be pursued.

First, perhaps we should consider the question, Are low unemployment, stable prices, and economic growth still important objectives in our society? Are we perhaps prepared to accept continuing rising prices with the economic and social damage they cause? Do we perhaps not feel the need for low unemployment in a generously financed welfare state? Do we perhaps think it would be better to have low economic growth or none at all, in the light of the prospective exhaustion of our resources and the growing pollution that economic growth has produced? Perhaps. As far as I can see, to project any of these to its logical conclusion would mean the end of democratic government and economic freedom—two of our most important values.

If, then, we are to try to continue to achieve low unemployment, stable prices, and economic growth, how do we go about doing it? The nostalgic answer is to explain away the depression of the 1930s and our more recent problems as being the result of government spending and misguided policy and to recommend a return to the 1926 faith in a self-correcting business system. Some would add proposals to slash government expenditures drastically, lower income tax rates, reduce their progressivity, and set an upper limit to the percentage of the GNP that government can spend. This approach is emotionally satisfying, especially to one who is disturbed by the speed of economic and social change. Life would be much simpler for such economists as were then employed. Unfortunately, I cannot imagine the proposals working successfully. They failed before, and conditions are less favorable for their success now. The political possibility of moving very far in this direction would appear to be nil.

What I think we do need is to take every feasible step to strengthen the self-correcting capacity of the economy so as to minimize the need for government intervention. I fear, however, that it is too late in the day to expect to achieve much along this line. Flexible adjustments of prices and wages in a downward direction are a rarity. Self-correcting mechanisms depend on the competition of numerous economic units performing the same services or functions. As the economic system has become more complex, there has been a great increase in the number of differentiated functions. These are "limiting factors"—points in the economic process at which a relatively small number of persons either acting cooperatively or taking "parallel action" can bring a major industry, or a city, to a grinding halt. Moreover, with the growth of "big business" and "big labor," the number of effective decision makers tends to decrease. Thus, the automaticity of competition gives way increasingly to the decisions of the few, whose motivations and behavior often can be understood and predicted better by psychologists or psychiatrists than by economists.

The second answer is to propose relying on fiscal and monetary policy and hoping for the best. I join fiscal and monetary policy together as one policy package and interpret it as being directed primarily to the management of consumer demand and investment demand. There is no space here to explore the fascinating controversy between those who emphasize fiscal policy and those who emphasize monetary policy. My conclusion is that each needs the other to be effective and that some monetarists, in particular, claim far more for their part of the package than it can possibly be expected to achieve. However, I consider fiscal and monetary policy to be the backbone of any program for economic stability and growth. Every feasible step should be taken to make it possible to use fiscal and monetary policy more effectively.

Fiscal policy has never been effectively applied against inflation. If, throughout the 1960s and 1970s, fiscal and monetary policy had been used with maximum effectiveness, we undoubtedly would not be in this inflationary spiral and could deal more readily with other problems. However, we are where we are. With an inflationary spiral going on virtually unabated, it must be noted that fiscal policy and monetary policy have little direct relevance in fighting the spiral, except that when they cause unemployment, or the fear of unemployment, they presumably reduce pressure for wage increases. This antiinflationary effect may be offset by a reduction in the supply of goods and services. The tax increases of the depression years, when they should not have taken place, were the last successful peacetime efforts to secure tax increases to fight inflation—although in the 1930s the inflation was only a fear, not a reality. The difficulties of increasing taxes in peacetime were recognized in the Treasury as early as 1945, and this in part accounts for the administration's resistance to proposals for tax reduction to meet the anticipated resumption of depression.

Fiscal policy has had considerable success in dealing with recessions and unemployment, but, as earlier discussion indicated, its usefulness is that of increasing general demand. However, it has little to offer in case of frictional, structural, or voluntary unemployment. In the present circumstances, there is little prospect of correcting the economic dilemma through fiscal and monetary action alone.

One reason for the failure to use fiscal policy more effectively is that Congress has no accepted guidelines around which to build a fiscal policy. To me, the concept of a balanced federal budget is a goal that should not be forgotten, although many economists appear to consider it of no significance. I find it difficult to understand why a soundly structured economy should need, in good years and bad years, the stimulation of government deficit spending, and I do not think such spending makes for a healthy economy, except as it prevents downward movements from cumulating and escalating. We have no budget-balancing concept to give fiscal discipline in the political field. The annually balanced budget was a politically powerful guideline, but was perverse economically and had to go. The "cyclically balanced budget," much in vogue in the early postwar years when it was promoted by the Committee for Economic Development and others, is considered by many economists to be too restrictive. Having escaped from the annually balanced budget, they want no other formula restrictions. The "full-employment balanced budget" in effect anticipates that with possible rare exceptions there will be a continuous, cumulative federal deficit, because the inevitable imbalances in the economy make it virtually certain that short of major war or other great emergency, full-employment production will never be realized without unacceptable inflation. And economists themselves are no great help; the impression is inescapable that almost every policy position has the support of at least one recognized economist to provide scholarly respectability.

Restraint on wage and price increases is necessary if the inflationary spiral is to be dampened and brought down to an acceptable level; this will require an incomes policy. To me, the maximum acceptable rate of inflation for the long run is one that is so small and so uncertain as not to enter into the planning of business, labor, and consumers. It will be extremely difficult to achieve that result, but once achieved it should be more easily maintained than any given higher rate of inflation, because in the latter case business and labor will seek and no doubt achieve increases in prices and wages sufficient to offset not only past inflation, but anticipated future inflation, thus pushing costs ahead at an accelerating rate. An incomes policy cannot be successful unless it is accepted and supported by organized labor and organized business. The obstacles to designing a program that will receive such acceptance are discouragingly great. The sudden imposition in August 1971, of a price and wage freeze, followed by controls, after years spent in condemning them, the administration of the controls by persons who did not believe in them, and their abandonment once the 1972 election was over have destroyed their usefulness for many years to come. Just as the fear of business reaction delayed for a long time the deliberate use of deficit spending during the 1930s, so today fear of preemptive price and wage increases threatens to paralyze the use of incomes policy.

Economists might help by mounting a vigorous educational campaign that pointed out the personal responsibility of every buyer and seller for the continuation of the inflationary spiral, with a view to arousing public condemnation of those who failed to cooperate in a voluntary incomes policy. Strong leadership by the administration, supported by congressional leaders, and acceptance by business and labor leaders would be required for such a campaign to be successful. Perhaps impossible, but worth trying.

We need a government jobs and training program to soak up some of the excessive unemployment, especially of those whose skills are inadequate for available jobs. The jobs programs of the 1930s, although ridiculed by many at the time as "leaf-raking," prevented a great deal of suffering, restored dignity to many who were alienated or had an undeserved sense of guilt, trained numerous individuals for private-sector jobs when they became available, and gave us a wealth of forests, buildings, books, works of art, statistical series, and other permanent contributions. The jobs part of the program should be viewed as a stopgap and not for permanent use. The program should, of course, be realistic in size and effectively administered. One danger is that in today's political climate, the wage scale might be set so high that the jobs of the program would be more attractive than numerous jobs in private industry.

These are all sensitive areas, but the most sensitive topic that I shall consider is planning. All economic units plan, with more or less success, but the idea that the U.S. government should plan for the economy has been anathema. Yet it is a logical step in a pluralistic concept of planning.[3] If every economic unit plans, the plans often support and reinforce one another; however, they may instead not lead to a balanced economy but rather, for example, to investment booms that greatly overexpand some types of facilities, along with failures to develop other sectors. Smooth coordination of private plans and their implementation are likely to require some large unit.

No sharply defined line between governmental policy and planning is likely to meet with common acceptance. To me, the stage of governmental planning is reached when the government makes quantitative forecasts and sets quantitative targets for various sectors of the national economy and proposes specific private and governmental action to achieve the targets. By this definition the federal government has long done a great deal of planning, although primarily with government funds—military spending, highways, development of rivers, harbors, and airports, and so on. Many regulatory agencies are engaged in planning, particularly in the form of restrictions. The critics of planning presumably have had in mind greater interference with private activities than these involve, perhaps considering general economic planning, whether as "central planning" or "indicative planning." The time may come when such general planning may be practicable, even necessary, but the experience of other countries is not reassuring.

The difficulties and dangers of planning are indeed sobering. The technical and administrative problems of planning are formidable even with such techniques as input-output analysis, the nation's economic budget, and computerized economic models. Securing compliance through information and persuasion are not likely to be enough. Tax incentives, loans, and subsidies are often relied on; they have the inbuilt political dangers of creating vested interests that make impossible later removal of the incentives, and of spreading the benefits to other sectors on grounds of equity, forgetting the original economic purpose. Another political danger is that planners will try to please everyone, resting on the illusion that there is plenty to go around. Such planning would exacerbate inflation and not reduce it.

Despite these concerns, I see no escape from an increased amount of governmental planning to supplement the pluralistic planning of private economic units in at least two sectors. One relates to dealing with the type of inflation that results from shortages and bottlenecks. In addition to large-scale worker training programs, better planning also is needed to avoid and eliminate bottlenecks and shortages in plant capacity and in the availability of raw materials, both of which reduce the feasibility of achieving low unemployment without inflation.

A second area where I think planning is going to be necessary is in connection with the proposed "New International Economic Order." I do not think that the United States can resist receiving a much larger volume of manufactures and semimanufactures from developing countries, since only through increased exports can they hope ever to repay the enormous debts they have incurred or to buy what they need for their further economic development. If the United States accepts these imports, it must prepare to do some restructuring of its own economy, as otherwise the imports will cause substantial domestic unemployment and business failures, since they are largely of types produced in less profitable industries with little margin for price competition. We cannot expect an individual wage or salary earner to create employment for himself; the best he can hope to do in the modern industrial world is to find a job if one is available. We cannot expect a manufacturer of a particular product who finds himself hard pressed by foreign competition to move out of the industry in which he has spent his life and start in another one that has both domestic and export potentialities. Nor can we expect any particular locality, heavily concentrated in one or a few industries, to reshape its industrial structure using only its own financial, intellectual, and market resources. This is a matter in which regional and national plans and programs will be necessary.

Accordingly, it is my view that government planning is needed in (1) dealing with sectoral shortages and bottlenecks in the supply of labor, plant capacity, and materials and (2) economic restructuring to permit the acceptance of more imports of manufactured products from the less developed countries.

Policies toward the less developed countries will involve multilateral negotiations and agreements, not only with the LDCs but also with other industrially advanced countries, which are facing the same type of problems that the United States is and which are its competitors. This calls attention to the international aspects of the whole economic policy problem, which are complex and require detailed examination not possible here. It is sufficient to state that the need to develop international cooperation is increasingly important because of growing inter-dependence—a result of advances in communications, transportation, the development needs of LDCs and the needs of all nations for fuels and minerals. The United States needs an international harmonization of economic policy. Otherwise, the equilibrium of the American economy is subject to being upset and U.S. economic policy to being frustrated by what happens abroad, while its actions may do unintended harm to foreign countries. Unfortunately, adding to the goals of national economic policy that of reaching international agreement requires a broader view of national interest than the United States or other governments have thus far been prepared to take.

A major addition to the types of federal intervention is welfare policy. As I indicated earlier, this started during the 1930s; by now it includes old age and survivors' insurance, unemployment insurance, public assistance, food stamps, Medicare, Medicaid, and dozens of other specific programs. They are "transfer payments" because either totally or partially the decision to spend is made by individuals and other private economic units, not by the government. One assumption of welfare policy is that the economic process does not distribute income among the popu-lation in accordance with the public interest and must be supplemented by redistribution through the political process. I have not discussed welfare policy as an approach to achieving "economic objectives" (that is, low unemployment, stable prices, economic growth) because these economic objectives have to do with production of income and not with its distribu-tion. Welfare programs, of course, are not unrelated to the economic process. On the one hand, they help sustain demand on an even keel, thus serving as one of the "automatic stabilizers" of fiscal policy. On the other hand, welfare programs may reduce the incentives of the recipients to accept employment that is not to their taste. If the welfare programs are financed by taxes, the incentives of investors, businessmen, and workers may be impaired; if financed by an expansion in the money supply, they are a potential inflationary factor, and this is to a lesser extent true also if they are financed by borrowing from the public. Welfare programs decrease the pressures to intervene in the economic process to force it to achieve directly a more acceptable pattern of income distribution.

As a concluding exercise, I wish to make a broad-brush comparison of the economic policy approaches previously discussed, as they relate to four points referred to earlier: self-corrective forces of the economic process, public patience to wait for these forces to work, effectiveness of public action, and comparative trust in the economic process and the political process.

Economic policy based on neoclassical economic theory assumes that the private economy is self-correcting in all significant respects and that the corrections will take place rapidly enough so that the public may be expected to wait patiently for them to occur. It is assumed further that it is far safer to trust the economic process than to resort to the political process, since public intervention would adversely affect the working of the automatic adjustment mechanism.

When monetary policy is added, the only necessary divergence from neoclassical assumptions of self-correction by the private economy is the recognition that to peform its traditional monetary functions government needs to set upper and lower limits to credit availability—a process that is somewhat erroneously called determining the supply of money. The role of the political process is only slightly increased, since the monetary instruments are impersonal and, superficiallly, do not involve favoring one sector of the economy as against another.

The addition of fiscal policy involves recognition that the unaided private economy may not provide adequate and stable demand necessary to achieve the "economic objectives." The role of the political process is substantially increased because it is not feasible to have an equal across-the-board increase or decrease in expenditures or taxes, since expenditures are made for specific purposes and taxes are levied on specific groups of people. However, the resource allocation function of the economic process operates freely within the resulting income and wealth pattern.

Adding incomes policy involves recognition that in at least some key industries competitive determination of prices and wages has been largely replaced by "price power" and "wage power" that can and sometimes do ignore conditions of supply and demand. Since incomes policy must be applied to particular groups, the role of the political process, including both legislation and administration, is substantially enlarged.

The addition of planning, even in the limited areas suggested above, injects the political process also into the supply side, on the assumption that the private economy will not produce with sufficient rapidity supplies in all sectors balanced to meet demand. This use of the political process is not parallel with the relation of fiscal policy to demand. In the fiscal policy case, the purpose is to affect the demand in the economy as a whole, whereas planning in relation to supply is focused on specific sectors that are deemed to be out of balance with requirements.

A combination of all of the above policy approaches places a heavy burden on the legislative and administrative institutions of government, which may not at this time be organized to handle the burden. However, there is no conceptual problem that makes using them to achieve the "economic objectives" impossible in a government run on the principle of one-man, one-vote.

An observer cannot be as optimistic about welfare policy in a one-man, one-vote democracy. All government services financed by taxation are to some extent redistributional, but redistribution is not ordinarily the objective in providing them and is as likely to be among individuals in similar income groups as from one income group to another. The objective of welfare policy, however, is the redistribution of income from higher income groups to lower income groups and other disadvantaged persons. There has, however, been a distinct trend toward making transfer payments to persons at higher income levels. Examples are subsidized middle-income housing and the sweetening of social insurance program benefits beyond those paid for by the insured groups, not to mention the long list of subsidies to agriculture and numerous industries.

Human desires are virtually unlimited. If the public were to conclude that these desires could be fulfilled by expanding such transfer payments, the demand would be very strong, adding new claims on an already over-claimed stream of national income. The public is misled as to the true cost and who pays it, and this must surely lead increasingly to the expectation that a person should receive more for less—that "redistribution" of income is not merely for the poverty-stricken and the unfortunate but for everyone. It is a corrupting trend likely to increase the threat of permanent inflation in a political democracy.

NOTES

1. For information on this section, see the economic reports of the president and the reports of the council; also Edwin G. Nourse, *Economics in the Public Service* (New York: Harcourt Publishing, 1953).

2. Gerhard Colm, ed., *The Employment Act Past and Future: A Tenth Anniversary Symposium* (Washington, D.C.: National Planning Association, 1956).

3. For my views on pluralistic planning, as of 1966, see Denis Munby, ed., *Economic Growth in World Perspective* (New York: Association Press, 1966), pp. 251–80.

4

THE BREAKDOWN OF
BRETTON WOODS
Hendrik S. Houthakker

I don't know if the editor of this volume wanted to have former advisers bare their breasts and confess their sins, but in any case that is what I will do, though it would take me much too long to confess all my sins. I left the government a little less confident in my judgment than I had been before. President Nixon once described his economic advisers as being often wrong but never in doubt, and if he had me in mind he had a point.

It may be interesting to discuss one specific development of which I had personal knowledge while in the government. As a member of the council, I was involved in problems ranging from copper pricing to farm policy, from supersonic transport to textiles, and in many others. In retrospect it seems clear that I was doing too many different things, far more than I could have any adequate knowledge of. My only excuse for staying with most of them anyway was that the other people involved often appeared to know even less than I did, or else had an axe to grind.

The most important matter in which I was not only involved but also had some understanding (however incomplete) of what was happening was the international monetary developments that led ultimately to the collapse of the Bretton Woods agreement in August 1971. The Bretton Woods agreement had been negotiated during World War II as the foundation for international monetary affairs in the postwar period. It

Revised version of a lecture given at Western Michigan University on November 18, 1976. Helpful comments on an earlier version were kindly provided by Arthur Burns, William Fellner, Gottfried Haberler, Walter Hoadley, Jacques Polak, Henry Reuss, Robert Solomon, Thomas Willett, and Paul Wonnacott; none of these is responsible for the remaining defects of this essay.

contained a detailed set of agreed rules for international conduct that the member countries undertook to obey. It also established two important institutions—the International Monetary Fund (IMF) and the International Bank for Reconstruction and Development (IBRD), both of which are still in existence. The Bretton Woods agreement was an attempt to combine the best features of the classic gold standard with the floating rates that had developed during the 1930s, while avoiding their worst features. By and large I still think that Bretton Woods was a great step forward and that its collapse was probably a misfortune for the world as a whole.

What I want to do in this essay is to retrace the story of its final stages, especially those aspects with which I was personally conversant. The full history of the demise of Bretton Woods has not yet been written, and I do not pretend to provide it here. Many of the relevant documents are not yet available, while an analysis of the statistics could hardly be attempted in this relatively brief essay. I hope that the recollections and judgments presented here will encourage and facilitate the writing of a more definitive history.

Let me recall further that the Bretton Woods agreement came into force a few years after the end of World War II and that from the beginning the United States had an important role in its operation. For a long time it was essentially something that the United States imposed on the rest of the world, not against its will, but nevertheless with a considerable exercise of pressure at certain times. One problem that emerged very soon in the postwar history of international monetary affairs was the so-called dollar problem, which took different forms at different times. Very early in the postwar period it appeared that other countries would be unable ever to balance their accounts with the United States because the dollar was so strong. This led to widespread concern among economists and policy makers, even though some of the customary balance of payments statistics suggest that there never really was a dollar shortage and that on the contrary the dollar became a currency of questionable strength almost as soon as the 1950s started. From 1950 through the early 1970s, the United States was in continuous external deficit by the usual standards, although it should be added that the standards by which weakness or strength of currencies are judged are often imperfect.

Nevertheless the fact is that the United States lost gold fairly continuously during the 1950s and 1960s. Initially this loss of gold was no problem at all. In the period before and during World War II, the United States for various reasons had wound up with nearly all of the world's gold, which did not make much sense. You can't play poker unless all the participants have at least some chips, so the redistribution of the U.S.

gold stock by itself was a desirable development. It was felt that after some years other countries would have rebuilt their gold reserves to more or less normal levels and that from then on the dollar would again be in a position where the United States would not be continuously running deficits. It did not turn out this way. Even after other countries had rebuilt their gold stocks, the United States continued to be in deficit according to the measures used in those days.

In the late 1950s, some worries started to emerge in Washington about this threat. Now, let me further explain that the Bretton Woods agreement was an agreement that involved a so-called adjustable peg. This meant that every currency, including the dollar, had a "par value" expressed in terms of gold. The actual exchange rate from day to day was allowed to fluctuate within a narrow band around this par value. The band in principle was equal to 1 percent. Thus the pound sterling, which had a par value of $2.80 for most of this period, could fluctuate between about $2.77 and about $2.83. It was the responsibility of each country to maintain the exchange rate within this narrow range by buying or selling its own currency. As a general rule, par values were fixed, but provisions were made in the agreement for adjusting ones that turned out to be unrealistic. This happened, for instance, with the British pound in 1949, when its value was reduced from $4.02 to the $2.80 referred to above.

In the late 1950s, it was realized in official circles that the dollar might also be subject to overvaluation—in other words, that the exchange value of the dollar was possibly unrealistic. At that time some thought was given to devaluation by the administration in Washington, but this idea was rejected, in part because of the dollar's peculiar and unique place in the international monetary system. A rather drastic measure such as devaluation, some feared, would be disturbing to world confidence and the harmonious development of world trade and finance. Others believed that the weakness of the dollar, which had only just become apparent, might pass in due course. So at that time the notion of devaluation was rejected, but these discussions did not reach the general public.[1]

Instead, the problems resulting from this continuing weakness of the dollar were dealt with in other ways, the most important of which was to create more liquidity. If there was a growing supply of international money, the United States could finance its deficit without perpetually running down its gold stock. One interpretation (perhaps somewhat unfair) of this solution is to compare the dollar with a boat that is attempting to pass down a river with many sand banks and other obstacles. Rather than adjusting the rudder, it was decided to pump more water into the river so that the boat would not run aground so often. This solution, adopted in the early 1960s, took a number of different forms. One form consisted of the so-called swap arrangements, more or less automatic credits that central banks give to each other. A whole network of swaps was arranged that enabled the different central banks to settle temporary surpluses or deficits without having to pay gold.

Another major innovation in international monetary cooperation that was negotiated during the 1960s was the creation of the Special Drawing Rights (SDRs). This international money, which still exists, is not the kind of foreign money you can buy when you go on a trip to Europe or to Mexico because SDRs cannot be used by private individuals or private firms. They were created out of thin air and serve only among central banks. This new form of liquidity was expected to eliminate, or at least reduce, the need for adjustment of exchange rates.

There was a third development that started at the time and that was even more important for subsequent history. This third development, which fitted in with the same phenomenom of increasing world liquidity, was the evolution of the Eurodollar market. Unlike the SDRs and the swaps, the Eurodollar market arose from private initiative rather than official planning. It did not involve central banks, but rather the commercial banks of the leading industrial nations. Curiously enough, the Eurodollar market had its origin with Soviet-owned banks in Western Europe, which were reluctant to hold dollars in the United States for fear that they might be expropriated. Therefore, they held dollars in European banks; these were the so-called Eurodollars, which subsequently had a tremendous expansion and are now a very large part of the world's money supply.

This expansion of liquidity did not succeed in sweeping the underlying problem under the rug. Some feeling remained that liquidity was not the right answer to what appeared to be an overvaluation of the dollar. The notion that the dollar was indeed overvalued spread rapidly in the early 1960s; economists such as Paul Samuelson, Randall Hinshaw, Jaroslav Vanek, and myself expressed it on a number of occasions. However, this view was at that time largely confined to academic circles and did not meet with any response in government circles. This was in part because the decision had been made recently, unbeknownst to the general public, that the dollar would not be devalued.

Academic talk about overvaluation was therefore not welcomed in official circles. It was not any more popular in Congress, and this is also of some importance for later developments. I myself argued that the dollar was overvalued in a paper[2] commissioned by the Joint Economic Committee of Congress, and particularly by its Subcommittee on International Economic Affairs. This subcommittee was then chaired by Henry Reuss, now chairman of the House Banking Committee, who has long been regarded as Congress's leading expert on international monetary affairs. But when there was a hearing on my paper before this subcommittee, the chairman was apparently so embarrassed by my statement that the dollar was overvalued that he did not ask me a single question. As we shall see, he swung radically to the other side later on.

What harm was actually being done by the overvalued dollar? Well, there were different kinds of harm, some of them more visible than others. One consequence was that the United States, in order to keep the balance of payments deficit under control, adopted a series of restrictions on international payments, contrary to its long-standing traditions of free capital movements. A number of such restrictions were introduced during the Kennedy administration, in particular, the Interest Equalization Tax. A further set of exchange controls, introduced under the Johnson administration on January 1, 1968, included fairly severe restrictions on direct investment by U.S. corporations and on lending by U.S. banks to foreigners. These restrictions by themselves were a distortion of efficient international finance and therefore involved some cost.

Perhaps more seriously, the overvaluation of the dollar during the 1960s led to an increase in protectionism on the part of the United States, supported particularly by the labor unions. The unions had been persuaded by Kennedy in 1962 to go along with the Trade Expansion Act, which was intended to liberalize world trade and in particular to secure U.S. participation in international trade negotiations. However, the argument used by the Kennedy administration to persuade the labor unions not to oppose liberal trade was most unfortunate. The labor unions were told that free trade is in the interest of U.S. workers because the United States exports more than it imports. This was a very superficial and misleading way of promoting free trade. Free trade is in the public interest, not because of exports but because of imports. Imports are the fruits of foreign trade, and exports are the cost of obtaining these fruits.

As happens frequently with misleading propaganda, it backfired on those who used it. In the early 1960s, the United States did have a sizable trade surplus, despite the overall weakness of its balance of payments as customarily measured. But as the dollar continued to be overvalued, the U.S. trade surplus shrank rapidly. Having been told that free trade is good because U.S. exports are greater than U.S. imports, the unions naturally concluded that free trade was bad when the opposite appeared to develop. So by the late 1960s, protectionism became a serious issue for Congress. A number of restrictive programs for particular industries had already been adopted starting in the early 1960s, and by the late 1960s protectionism appeared to have the upper hand. The Mills bill, introduced when Wilbur Mills was at the height of his congressional power and providing for quotas on many imports into the United States, was a very serious threat, especially when it gained administration support in the summer of 1970. Its enactment was averted only by delicate maneuvering on the part of a handful of free traders in Congress, in the administration, and in the private sector. But that is another story.

This then was the background at the point where I myself became more directly involved in international economic policy. In 1967–68 I was on the staff of the CEA, which had become increasingly interested in alternatives to exchange controls. During my stay, I worked, among other things, on methods of making exchange rates more flexible within the Bretton Woods framework[3] and made a presentation on this subject at the U.S. Treasury, where interest in reform was also beginning to stir. Before the 1968 presidential election, a task force was set up by the Republicans under the chairmanship of Gottfried Haberler, then my colleague at Harvard University and now at the American Enterprise Institute. This task force was one of several under the general direction of Paul McCracken, subsequently chairman of the Council of Economic Advisers and also a contributor to this volume. The Haberler task force was concerned with international monetary affairs and took a more fundamental look at the U.S. financial predicament than had been done for quite some time. The members of the task force included, apart from Haberler and myself, William Fellner, who was a professor at Yale at that time and later became a member of the CEA; Henry Wallich, then also at Yale and now a member of the board of governors of the Federal Reserve System; and Wilson Schmidt of the Virginia Polytechnic Institute, subsequently at the Treasury. It also included two distinguished bank economists, Walter Hoadley of the Bank of America and Tilford Gaines of Manufacturers Hanover Trust Company. The group's secretary, who took an active part in the discussions, was Thomas Willett, at that time assistant professor at Harvard, now at the Treasury.

This group was, to begin with, concerned about the increasing reliance on exchange controls of various kinds that had evolved during the Kennedy and Johnson administrations. It was even more alarmed by the gradual spread of protectionism, which it also considered to be contrary to the national interest. The group agreed that the value of the dollar in relation to other currencies had to be reduced. U.S. exports had to be made more competitive with those of other countries and U.S. imports had to be curtailed, not by artificial restrictions or by creating a recession but by making them more expensive through a devaluation.

The Haberler task force gave much thought to how this desired result should be brought about. By that time it was generally believed that other countries would not agree to an outright devaluation of the dollar. In fact they were thought to be inalterably opposed to it, partly as a result of American propaganda. As mentioned earlier, the Bretton Woods agreement provided for adjustments in par values if they turned out to be unrealistic, and this had been done in such cases as the devaluations of sterling in 1949 and 1967. Actually, there had not been many adjustments in major currencies; between 1961 and 1967 there were none at all. Gradually, tacit agreement had emerged among the central banks and finance ministers of the world that the devaluation clause of the Bretton Woods agreement should not be used because it was disruptive and would lead to speculation.[4] Instead of the adjustable peg envisaged by the Bretton Woods agreement, the United States should have "fixed and immutable exchange rates," a phrase much used by U.S. Treasury officials during the early 1960s. In other words, the exchange rate adjustment clause of the Bretton Woods agreement had been set aside, though the 1967 devaluation of sterling could not be prevented. This, of course, made it very difficult for the United States to talk about changes in exchange rates, if only because U.S. officials had been most insistent that the dollar would never be devalued; they had never tired of repeating that the dollar was "as good as gold." This background was relevant to the strategy that the Haberler task force proposed in order to bring about the needed adjustment in the external value of the dollar.

What the Haberler task force recommended, in effect, was that other countries should be faced with a choice of either holding larger and larger amounts of dollars or letting their own exchange rates appreciate, which would have the same effect as a depreciation of the dollar. This meant that conversion of surplus dollars into gold had to be made more difficult, though there was some disagreement in the task force as to the time when the dollar should be made formally inconvertible. In any case, it was expected that most countries would sooner or later opt for an exchange rate adjustment as the lesser of the two evils facing them. This strategy later became known as "benign neglect"—a phrase that came from an entirely different area. It had earlier been applied by Daniel Patrick Moynihan, now Senator Moynihan, to the question of discrimination against minorities. The phrase "benign neglect" also became common in international monetary affairs, especially after Haberler and Willett wrote a joint paper in 1971,[5] which to a large extent reflected the Haberler task force report.

A further item of great concern to the Haberler task force was the increasing rigidity of the Bretton Woods framework due to the setting-aside of the exchange rate adjustment clause. A system can only work if it can adapt itself to changing circumstances. In the case of international monetary affairs, this meant that exchange rates can be changed when necessary. If you don't allow that, you are left with a straitjacket, which sooner or later will be torn apart. So the Haberler task force recommended the restoration of a suitable degree of flexibility to the Bretton Woods agreement. Some members were sympathetic to freely floating rates, but there was also much concern that the adoption of floating rates might jeopardize the great progress that had been made in previous years in world trade and world finance. The 1950s and 1960s had indeed been an impressive period in terms of international expansion. World trade grew at an unprecedented rate and so did international capital movements. These were not achievements to be lightly dismissed. Therefore, another recommendation of the Haberler report (along with dismantling controls and "benign neglect") was to improve the Bretton Woods system rather than to throw it away.

The Haberler report was never formally adopted. It was submitted to President Nixon after his election, but I don't know whether he ever read it. He had no strong interest in international monetary affairs, as shown by an incident recorded on the Watergate tapes when H. R. Haldeman comes in and wants to tell him about the Italian lira; his response was "[expletive deleted] the Italian lira!" His foreign policy adviser Henry Kissinger also had his mind on less mundane matters.

Nevertheless, the Haberler report had considerable influence on policy. To show this, let me first say something about the organization of international monetary policy at that time. International monetary affairs had for some years been directed by a small interagency group chaired by the undersecretary of the Treasury for Monetary Affairs, who had the final word. When the Nixon administration took over in 1969, the chairmanship was assumed by Paul Volcker, who is now president of the Federal Reserve Bank of New York. Thus the group became known as the Volcker group. It consisted, apart from Volcker himself and a few other Treasury officials, of representatives from the State Department, the Federal Reserve Board, the National Security Council, and the Council of Economic Advisers. I myself served on the Volcker group during the time I was a member of the council from January 1969 to July 1971; the termination date is important to my story, as will become evident. Each of the agency representatives also had a deputy; in the council's case, this was first Paul Wonnacott and later Marina Whitman. This group met quite frequently, on the average perhaps twice a week. It was responsible, apart from day-to-day consideration of international monetary matters, for developing a long-run policy. Its recommendations on long-run policy, submitted to the president in or around May 1969, did not reflect the Haberler report completely, but they had much in common with it.

Apart from myself, the member of the Volcker group with the greatest sympathy for the Haberler approach was Fred Bergsten, who was in charge of economic affairs at the National Security Council. Since Henry Kissinger knew little about international monetary matters and cared less, Bergsten could speak with the authority of Henry Kissinger without having to check back with him. Volcker himself was skeptical about the Haberler recommendations, but was focusing almost entirely on short-term problems. So were most of the group's other members with the notable exception of William Dale, who was then the U.S. executive director of the IMF and recognized the need for reform of Bretton Woods.

Even so, the policy of "benign neglect" coincided to a large extent with the policy subsequently followed, though in a rather indirect way because it had never been formally agreed upon. It is true that there was a meeting involving the president, Kissinger, Arthur Burns, Paul McCracken, and various other people (including me) at the White House in June 1969, which adopted the long-run recommendations of the Volcker group. But, even there, some questions remained as to what really was decided. This is unfortunately typical of such meetings; everybody goes away with a different idea as to the outcome—usually what he or she would have liked to hear.* Those who favored benign neglect saw it as an endorsement of their view, but one person who apparently did not was the chairman of the group himself, Paul Volcker. A highly intelligent and forceful individual with great knowledge of international finance, he acted throughout more as a negotiator with his mind on the next international meeting than as a policy maker.† He felt that ideas on long-run reform should remain in the academic sphere, and said so publicly.

Inevitably, however, occasions arose in which the new policy became manifest. The first one of these was shortly after the start of the Nixon administration—in early April 1969 to be precise. We have already seen that the Johnson administration had introduced strict controls on direct investment abroad by U.S. corporations. These controls were unpopular with business, which rightly considered them a distortion of their normal financial operations. Some corporations that in the past had not borrowed at all were forced to place bonds in other countries contrary to their normal financial policy. So there was great pressure from business to relax this program. The Volcker group was responsive to this pressure, not only out of sympathy for business and out of aversion to controls generally, but also because U.S. controls reduced the need for other countries to correct their surpluses. At that time, the U.S. balance of payments, which had not been very good, was gradually deteriorating. Things became worse later on, but they certainly were not good in early

---

*One issue that was settled at this meeting was the official price of gold. The Haberler report did not favor an increase in the gold price, except possibly as part of a bargain with the Europeans to apprciate their currencies; this possibility was never explored. At the White House meeting, Arthur Burns, then counselor to the president, suggested a higher gold price, but he did not prevail.

†He may well have agreed with the late Dean Acheson, reported to have said, "I don't care who makes the policy, provided I can do the negotiating." It may be relevant to add that Volcker had served his Treasury apprenticeship during the heyday of fixed exchange rates in the middle 1960s.

1969. The Johnson administration might have chosen this opportunity to further tighten the exchange controls amidst strident declarations that the dollar would not be devalued in any circumstances. What the Nixon administration did in April 1969, on the contrary, was quite significant: it relaxed the controls in the face of a deteriorating balance of payments. It thereby signaled to anybody who was listening that the United States was not going to follow the previous policy but was switching course.*

It is not clear how many people realized it at the time. Later that month I went on a trip to Europe as a member of an important mission that visited a number of European capitals. The first place we went was Brussels, the headquarters of the European Economic Community (EEC). Although our discussions were mostly on trade problems I also had occasion to talk with the official in charge of international monetary affairs at the EEC, Ugo Mosca. I asked him what Europe would do if the dollar were devalued under the rules of Bretton Woods. He stated flatly that all European currencies would be devalued by the same percentage on the same day.* This, of course would have made U.S. devaluation ineffective, because there would be no change in the relative exchange rate. His response confirmed what the Haberler task force had assumed, namely that other countries were not prepared to see the dollar devalued.

On this same trip I also talked with a number of central bankers in various countries, in seven or eight countries altogether. After the discouraging reaction from the EEC, the question of devaluation was not raised again, but we did discuss another important item on the Haberler agenda, namely the improvement of the Bretton Woods system. In a lecture at the University of Bonn, I pointed out that, in the same proclamation in which the president relaxed exchange controls, he had also called for international monetary reform, and I presented some ideas on how this could be accomplished.

The conventional wisdom at the U.S. Treasury had been that the Europeans and the Japanese did not want to see the Bretton Woods system made more flexible and thus more capable of adjusting to changing circumstances. This belief may have been correct in the case of some countries, but not all. When the subject was brought up to them, two eminent central bankers expressed strong interest in reform of the Bretton Woods system; these were Dr. Otmar Emminger of the German Bundesbank and Guido Carli, then governor of the Bank of Italy. These two gentlemen did recognize the problem, and their views were important because they were recognized leaders in central banking. Immediately after my meeting with Carli in Rome, I sent a long cable to Paul Volcker

---

*Actually the dollar subsequently had a temporary period of technical strength resulting from a more stringent domestic monetary policy.

†Such a reaction would have been in violation of the Bretton Woods agreement, which prohibited competitive devaluation.

telling him that Treasury's impressions about the European attitude toward reform of Bretton Woods were mistaken, at least in the case of Germany and Italy. Other central bankers, while less enthusiastic, did not appear to be opposed either.

The apparent interest in reform led to further study of improved flexibility of exchange rates within the Bretton Woods system. A number of difficult technical questions had to be resolved. The Volcker group initiated a series of consultations with other countries centering on the concept of the "crawling peg." This was one way of making exchange rates somewhat more flexible without violating the basic concepts of Bretton Woods. These bilateral technical discussions were followed by a more formal exercise at the IMF, where the executive directors, each of whom represents one or more countries, attempted to devise suitable amendments to the Bretton Woods agreement. They did not succeed in time, as we shall see, but the momentum did seem to be there.

In the meantime, the United States became more and more reluctant to sell gold in exchange for foreign-held dollars, an obligation that it had accepted when the Bretton Woods agreement went into force shortly after World War II. The United States was supposed to make its gold available without limit to other countries for monetary purposes, but in fact it increasingly discouraged other countries from asking for gold.* I am not sure if the United States ever actually told any country that they couldn't have it, but it was made clear to them that such requests were not welcome, to say the least, and most of them took the hint. They did not ask for gold when they had accumulated dollars, as they had done previously; instead they held these dollars as an investment—perhaps an involuntary investment. And this, of course, was the essence of "benign neglect."

The policy of "benign neglect" accomplished much, though not enough. Two countries that were of particular concern to the United States did allow their currencies to appreciate. Germany had a formal revaluation in the fall of 1969 followed in 1971 by a float of the German mark, which led to similar action by other European nations. Canada in May 1970 went back to the floating rate on which it had been until 1962 but which had subsequently been abandoned. As a result the Canadian dollar, which of course accounts for a large part of U.S. trade, appreciated ultimately by some 10 percent.

---

*This policy actually had been initiated before 1969, particularly with respect to Germany. To underscore this point, the United States returned some gold to the International Monetary Fund in 1970. This gold had been borrowed by the United States some years earlier, partly to make its reserves look larger and partly to provide the IMF with interest income. By 1970, both these objectives had become obsolete.

These two adjustments in fact left only one major problem, namely Japan. We believed the Japanese yen to be grossly undervalued with respect to the U.S. dollar and made this belief known to the Japanese in various ways, though at times the signals from the United States may have been conflicting.* It has occasionally been suggested that the Japanese never realized that the United States wanted them to revalue, but it would be more correct to say that the Japanese preferred not to hear.† They were happy with their undervalued currency, which gave them a tremendous volume of exports. The Japanese were (and perhaps still are) great believers in "export-led growth"; the large growth in their exports meant a high rate of growth for the country as a whole. It is a dubious proposition because they were in effect giving some of their exports away; the imports they got in return were not commensurate with the value of these exports. Nevertheless, the Japanese did not want to hear about any adjustment in the value of the yen. The large growth in Japanese exports was also an important stimulant to the rising U.S. protectionism.

At this point in my story I have come to early 1971, when John Connally became secretary of the Treasury. This may have been a turning point in international financial affairs. I say "may have been" because it is always tempting to interpret history in terms of personalities while overlooking the fundamentals. Future analysis may well show that the underlying cause of the August 1971 crisis was the reversal in monetary policy that took place earlier in that year. The 1969–70 recession had kept the dollar relatively strong, but it had also caused some unemployment, and the credit squeeze had to be abandoned. This in turn made the dollar less attractive to foreigners and capital started to flow out of the United States.

However this may be, the appointment of Connally certainly caused a difference in style. A quick-witted and persuasive wheeler-dealer, he was not in the least intimidated by his lack of background in financial matters; in fact he felt little need to consult Volcker or other experts on his staff. I must leave it to the experts to decide whether his reputation of being a top-notch politician is borne out by the facts, but there can be no doubt that Nixon (no tyro at politics himself) held him in the highest regard. So he saw the president very frequently, in effect becoming his principal political adviser.

---

*In the spring of 1971, for instance, Philip Trezise (then assistant secretary of state for economic affairs) went to Tokyo with this message, but it was subsequently disavowed by Treasury officials.

†Japan was also the only country that turned down the American invitation to participate in the bilateral technical discussions on exchange rate flexibility referred to earlier.

I cannot say for sure what advice Connally gave, since their meetings were private and have not been described by either participant; all we know is that Connally urged Nixon to ingratiate himself with such questionable allies as the dairy lobby. It may be surmised that in addition Connally told Nixon he should be seen doing things that would make favorable headlines. In the first few years of his administration, Nixon was not a particularly active president. He was of course deeply interested in foreign affairs, and we now know that in those days he was bringing about the famous detente with the Soviet Union and China, but all this had to be done in secret, so he got no credit at the time. Furthermore, his domestic economic policy was not going to the public's satisfaction. Worst of all, liquidating the war in Vietnam took longer than he had expected, and its extension to Cambodia caused a storm of protest. If there had been an election in 1971 Nixon would almost certainly have been defeated. So John Connally probably told him that this was not the way for a president to stay in office. Whether it was Connally's advice or not, Nixon became gradually converted to a more activist aproach.

Developments in another branch of the government were also relevant to the unfolding crisis. Let us return to Congressman Henry Reuss, who was still chairing the only congressional committee that took a continuing interest in international monetary affairs. In the spring of 1971, there were hearings before Congressman Reuss, who, together with Senator Jacob Javits, had proposed an international conference to discuss exchange rates. There were many witnesses, the most important one being Paul Volcker. His testimony contained little or nothing to reassure Reuss, who has been a consistent champion of an open world economy. It blamed the growing speculation on the Eurodollar market and failed to outline any credible policy. Even allowing for Volcker's natural reluctance to rock the boat during the gathering storm, he can hardly be said to have risen to the occasion—perhaps because Connally did not want him to.

In my own testimony I told the committee just what I have written here, that the appreciation of the Canadian and German currencies was an important step forward in correcting the overvaluation of the dollar and that the principal currency still to be adjusted was the yen. (This statement, of course, was addressed as much to Japan as to the subcommittee.)[6] If those three exchange rates were all adjusted, then the United States would not have to worry about the other ones, many of which would follow suit. In other words, I implied that "benign neglect" was working, though perhaps slowly. My remarks also had to be circumspect, and their authority was reduced by public knowledge of my impending departure from the administration.

The upshot of the hearings was that Reuss persisted in his idea of an international conference. Coming from an influential congressman of the majority party, this was an inflammatory proposal. International monetary conferences have been occasions for widespread and rampant speculation, the conference at Bonn in 1968 being the prime example. Once such a conference is announced, all sorts of rumors spread and billions of dollars will change hands in the course of a few hours. So the Reuss-Javits proposal, which to my mind reflected a misinterpretation of the situation at that time, contributed to the growing instability of the foreign exchange markets. Until the beginning of 1971, these markets had been relatively stable. Foreign countries did accumulate dollars continuously, but there was no massive speculation. That did not start in earnest until after the Reuss-Javits statement, which was followed by a report calling more explicitly for a realignment of exchange rates.

Now back to Connally, whose "machismo" was apparently aroused by an event that may or may not have been significant in itself. It is one of those minor mysteries of history that, like many events I have described from my own recollections, may one day be clarified when various people write their memoirs and the relevant documents are published. But the event itself is not in doubt, namely, that in early August 1971 the British inquired about the possibility of gold cover for their dollar holdings. The Bank of England held fairly sizable dollar reserves and was obviously afraid that the dollar might be devalued. In order to prevent a capital loss, the British wanted their dollars guaranteed at their gold value.

To Treasury officials in Washington, one of whom told me about it a few days later, this was a low blow. The United States had gone to great lengths to defend the pound sterling, especially in 1964. In 1967, this rather futile exercise could not be successfully repeated, and the pound sterling was actually devalued. Still, we had always been ready to help Britain, so when the Bank of England expressed distrust of the dollar, one can readily imagine that Connally and some of his collaborators were incensed.* Connally himself, at the subsequent meeting at Camp David, referred to the British request (which was at least partially agreed to) as a sign that the international monetary situation was rapidly falling apart. It may have been the last straw as far as he was concerned. After a weekend meeting at Camp David between Nixon and Connally ending on August 15, 1971, the United States decided formally to sever the link between the dollar and gold, thus bringing the Bretton Woods agreement to an end.

---

*British commentators[7] have attempted to reduce the Bank of England's inquiry to a mere technicality. This interpretation would imply that the British monetary authorities had suddenly lost all the *savoir faire* built up over centuries of experience.

The August 15 decision was part of a larger package that included domestic components of great importance. Central to the entire program was a plan to accelerate the recovery from the 1969–71 recession by tax measures.* This raised the danger of renewed inflation, which was to be counteracted by a wage-price freeze as a prelude to a comprehensive system of wage-price controls. Stronger domestic growth was also likely to aggravate the deficit in the balance of payments, and the suspension of convertibility could be interpreted as a response to that threat, though of course it had much wider imlications. Finally, a temporary import surcharge of 10 percent was imposed, presumably as an indication to other countries concerning the amount of exchange rate adjustment we considered necessary. In this essay I have not said much about the domestic aspects of international monetary policy because until August 1971 they had not been critical to the outcome. The assembly of the August 15 package was motivated in part by the political problems mentioned earlier; it enabled Nixon to present a New Economic Policy, which became considerably more popular than the old one and helped secure his 1972 reelection.

Subsequent international developments are not part of my story here.† Let me just recall that a general realignment of par values was achieved after a few months in which the dollar depreciated by approximately the desired figure of 10 percent. To that extent, U.S. policy had been successful, though at the expense of the international monetary system. A feeble attempt to resurrect the fixed rates with the Smithsonian agreement of December 1971 did not last long because it lacked the necessary structural reforms. In early 1973 all the major currencies of the world went on a floating rate, thus destroying the last resemblance with Bretton Woods and confirming that August 15 could not be reversed.

One question I want to raise about the final outcome is, Was it necessary? To put the question differently, Did the U.S. government panic? Could it have held out longer? Obviously, it is hard to be certain because some of the facts of the situation are still not known, but my guess is that the U.S. government could not have held out much longer

---

*It was probably because of this basic intention that Arthur Burns's objections at Camp David to the closing of the gold window were overruled.[8] Burns wanted to protect the dollar by cutting government expenditures, contrary to the acceleration plan.

†I left the CEA on July 15, 1971 because I had exhausted my leave from Harvard and did not want to abandon my academic career. At that time the monetary turmoil had already become intense, but no plans to terminate Bretton Woods had been made to my knowledge. Fred Bergsten, the other main advocate of "benign neglect" in the Volcker group, had left the administration shortly before me.

after the statements made by Henry Reuss and others had unleashed enormous capital movements. It is not clear whether benign neglect would ultimately have persuaded the Japanese to revalue the yen. Indeed, even after August 15, they held out for some more months, in the face of massive speculation, before they finally gave in to the inevitable.

We must recognize also that the policy of benign neglect in the end had a heavy cost. The huge build-up of dollar holdings by other countries added to the world's money supply and thereby provided fuel for the great inflation of 1972–74, though it may not have been the only cause.[9] This should have been foreseen by the advocates of benign neglect, myself included. I never expected benign neglect to take such a long time to accomplish its purpose. This accumulation of world reserves, most of which actually came after August 15, came on top of the new international liquidity decided upon in the 1960s (SDRs and swap agreements), and in addition there was the rapid development of Eurodollars. By the early 1970s, the world was awash with excess liquidity, which helped bring about the 1972–74 inflation and the ensuing recession, from neither of which the world has fully recovered so far. In retrospect, one must wonder, therefore, if benign neglect was a wise policy.

What were the alternatives? One was intensified use of exchange controls, following the example of the two preceding administrations. A Republican president, devoted (at least until August 1971) to a free economy and dependent on the support of business, could hardly have embraced that approach, and its long-term effectiveness is in any case open to serious doubt. Another possibility was a restrictive economic policy with a view to reducing or reversing the external deficit. This was actually tried in 1969–70 (though primarily to curtail domestic inflation), and in 1970 some measures of the balance of payments did show an improvement over previous years, but popular reaction soon demonstrated how limited the potential for such a policy was. Finally, the dollar could have been devalued outright, as I proposed in 1962. Because of European and Japanese opposition, this would have called for difficult negotiations, but in the end it might have been less disruptive than the course actually pursued and might have preserved the essentials of the existing monetary system. This third approach was never considered seriously until it was too late.*

---

*It was suggested on at least two occasions in 1971 by Pierre-Paul Schweizer of the International Monetary Fund. The only immediate result was to make him *persona non grata* at the U.S. Treasury. At the Smithsonian agreement, the U.S. dollar was devalued, contrary to the strong stand taken initially by Secretary Connally.

It was particularly unfortunate that in the period surveyed here international monetary reform, another recommendation of the Haberler task force, did not get anywhere. The Bretton Woods system was not repaired. The rigidity that implied its doom remained until the bitter end; Canada and Germany escaped it only by going to floating rates in violation of Bretton Woods. If international monetary reform had been agreed upon anytime before August 15, the breakdown might have been avoided, but there was no sufficient sense of urgency. In that respect, some of the blame lies with the IMF, an organization that itself had been set up by the Bretton Woods agreement. The fund was headed at that time by Pierre-Paul Schweizer, who (judging from public statements and private conversations) failed to realize the need for international monetary reform, especially in the area of exchange rates. He saw the system for which he was responsible break down without issuing the clarion call that could have saved it. His principal assistants were too committed to the prevailing interpretation of the details of the IMF charter to look favorably on significant amendments; in effect, they could not see the Bretton Woods for the Bretton trees. Unless a system is periodically rejuvenated, it will die.

Mindful that the title of this volume includes the words "Economic Advice," I will finally draw some conclusions, in the first place for international monetary policy, a subject that is no longer much in the news. We no longer have an international monetary system; instead there is a regime of floating rates, with frequent intervention by most central banks. There are no rules than can be violated, despite recent attempts by the IMF to bring its charter up to date—about five years too late. By the same token, there are no rules on which international business can build reliable expectations for the future. Exchange rates have fluctuated sharply, sometimes for no obvious reason, and these fluctuations have already played havoc with the accounts of firms operating in more than one country. The growth of international trade appears to have slowed down, possibly due in part to cyclical factors.

Yet it would be highly premature to condemn the present system as a failure. The danger of a return to the chaos of the 1930s, with its proliferation of exchange controls and protectionist measures, has so far been avoided. International economic cooperation, spurred by acute awareness of interdependence, is still active. Even the shock to the world economy caused by higher oil prices has been largely overcome. Apparently the world is learning to live with managed floating. Nevertheless I believe that in the longer run we shall need a more explicit framework for international financial transactions than we have now. As long as nearly all countries suffer from an unprecedented combination of substantial unemployment and continuing inflation it would be short-sighted to pretend that all is well. The search for an international monetary system more flexible than Bretton Woods, yet capable of providing comparable stability, should continue.

My second conclusion has to do with the management of economic policy. There are many reasons why the U.S. approach to international monetary problems before August 15 turned out to be unnecessarily disruptive in the end; one of these reasons was excessive secrecy. Not nearly enough was done to tell the press and the public what was being done, and why. Even some people who should have known were left in the dark; Congressman Reuss, whose role in the final collapse of Bretton Woods was discussed earlier, was probably in this category.* Now it is true that the administration's approach was kept secret in part because some of the main participants did not fully support it; Paul Volcker, for instance, often made statements that were at best ambiguous, as did successive secretaries of the Treasury. It is also true that international finance has traditionally been treated as something only the initiated should know about, for fear of speculation or worse. At the same time, this lack of general understanding was ultimately detrimental. In any democracy it is difficult to carry out policies without public awareness, public criticism, and public cooperation wherever possible.† Under the U.S. Constitution, congressional involvement is even more essential, no matter how time-consuming and politically hazardous. As regards speculation, it is ironic that the policy pursued in 1969–71, carried out with all possible precautions in this respect, ended in the largest short-term capital movements the world has ever seen. It is fortunate indeed that the habits of secrecy endemic in the Johnson-Nixon years have given way to greater openness under their successors, Gerald Ford and Jimmy Carter.

My last observation refers to the CEA, to which all contributors to this volume have belonged at one time or another—an experience, I may add, that changes one's way of thinking permanently. The council's main

---

*A rather more curious case is Charles Coombs, who as Vice President of the New York Federal Reserve Bank was in charge of official U.S. transactions in foreign exchange. According to his recent book, *The Arena of International Finance* (New York: Wiley-Interscience, 1976) he never knew what U.S. official policy was, or indeed that there was one. Yet the Federal Reserve Board was strongly represented in the Volcker group. Can it be that the board did not talk with the New York Fed? Or was Coombs told, but, like the Japanese mentioned earlier, did not want to hear?

†While a member of the council I made a number of speeches on international monetary matters, but the text had to be approved by others members of the Volcker group and therefore tended to blandness.

function, of course, is to watch over domestic fiscal and monetary policy, but as Paul McCracken emphasized in his essay, there is more to that than meets the eye. International economic policy is an important concern not only because it affects the domestic economy, but also because it calls for a degree of economic analysis that the operating agencies (particularly Treasury) are not always willing or able to provide, overwhelmed as they are by day-to-day responsibilities and sometimes by fixed policy positions. The council's problems with Treasury* are therefore different from those with the "client agencies" such as Agriculture and Labor, which are forever trying to do something for their constituents without necessarily taking the public interest into account. It is no accident that the council has often been able to introduce a fresh point of view where the operating agencies tend to get into a rut. The council also has its own window on the outside world because its chairman heads the U.S. delegation to the Economic Policy Committee of the Organization for Economic Cooperation and Development.

Thus it was the council, under Paul McCracken's leadership, that pressed hardest for international monetary reform against the skepticism of most other agencies. Although this effort was not successful in time, it could have averted the breakdown of Bretton Woods and at least some of the subsequent gyrations in the world economy. What I would advise now is that the council continue its independent assessment of international economic developments, unencumbered by the dogmatism that in the past has sometimes paralyzed the other government departments in this vital area.

NOTES

1. For details, see Robert Solomon, *The International Monetary System 1945–1976: An Insider's View* (New York: Harper and Row, 1977), pp. 38–40. This valuable book was not yet available at the time of my 1976 lecture.

2. "Exchange Rate Adjustment," in U.S. Congress, Joint Economic Committee, *Factors Affecting the U.S. Balance of Payments*, 87th Cong., 2d Sess., 1962. Some of the arguments in this paper have been criticized, and rightly so, but the main conclusion appears to have been widely accepted.

---

*A minor illustration occurred when I was on the council staff in 1967–68 and felt that the annual report should for the first time say something about a significant development in international finance, the Eurodollar market. With the council's encouragement I drafted a descriptive paragraph, but Treasury prevented its publication, apparently because any mention of private international liquidity might undercut its campaign for additional official liquidity. Needless to say when I became a member, the Eurodollar market was discussed in the report.

3. Some of the results are in my article, "The Future of the International Monetary System," *Economic Quarterly Review* (Amsterdam-Rotterdam Ban), December 1968.

4. Evidence on this point can also be found in Solomon, op. cit., ch. 3.

5. G. Haberler and T. Willett, *A Strategy for U.S. Balance-of-Payment Policy* (Washington, D.C.: American Enterprise Institute, 1971).

6. For these hearings, see U.S. Congress, Joint Economic Committee, Subcommittee on International Exchange and Payments, *The Balance of Payments Mess*, June 16, 17, 21, 23, and 24, 1971.

7. For instance, Henry Brandon, *The Retreat of American Power* (New York: Doubleday, 1973).

8. Reported in William Safire, *Before the Fall* (New York: Doubleday, 1975).

9. For alternative views see Solomon, op. cit., ch. 15, and T. D. Willett, "The Euro-currency Market, Exchange-Rate Systems, and National Financial Policies," in Carl H. Stem, John H. Makin, and Dennis E. Logue, eds., *Eurocurrencies and the International Monetary System* (Washington, D.C.: American Enterprise Institute, 1976).

5

CURRENT POLICY IN
A LONG-TERM CONTEXT

James S. Duesenberry

In the years since World War II, we have acquired a lot of experience in the making of fiscal and monetary policy. It remains to be seen whether that experience has taught us wisdom and good judgment. It is clear that much of what we thought we knew has proved to be at least partly wrong. The Employment Act of 1946 was passed just 31 years ago. It may be significant that the 20th anniversary of the act—in February 1966—was celebrated with a big party at the Brookings Institution, while the 25th and 30th anniversaries passed unnoticed.

The Employment Act that set up the CEA symbolized a general conviction that the United States ought never to allow a recurrence of the great depression of the 1930s. More generally it reflected the widespread view that the booms, panics, and depressions that had marred the history of industrial countries were unnecessary and could be controlled by proper government policy. That view was not exclusively or even primarily an American one. Indeed it was accepted almost universally in the market-oriented industrial countries. The economic instability of the past—at least in peacetime—was generally attributed to the inherent instability of the private sector. The remedy was to offset the fluctuations generated by the private sector by government action. The instrument was contracyclical fiscal policy with the emphasis on the use of public works programs. After the experience of the 1930s, monetary policy was regarded as ineffective. Some thought it might be useful as a restrictive instrument, but the phrase "pushing on a string" epitomizes a widespread belief in the ineffectiveness of monetary policy for inducing expansion. Variation in taxes was generally thought to be politically impractical. To complete my brief and probably unfair summary, it will be noted that I have hardly alluded to inflation. The proponents of the Employment Act did not dwell on inflation even though 1946 was hardly a year of price stability. The opponents of the act had quite a bit to say about inflation. Indeed they said enough to change the title of the act and a good deal of its substance. The original bill was to use the term "Full Employment" in the title and was to have contained a much more definite commitment to specific employment goals than the Employment Act, which mandated the pursuit of "maximum employment, production, and purchasing power." It is one of the beauties of the English language as used in politics that everyone understood that "full" employment was more than "maximum" employment.

The opponents of a firm commitment to employment targets feared that such a commitment would be inflationary because the government would be overzealous in carrying out the act's objectives and because they feared that trade unions would force up wages without fear of the consequences because of the full-employment guarantee.

As it has turned out, all the parties to these controversies were wide of the mark in many respects. The sources of instability turned out to be more governmental than private. In the last 30 years, the most destabilizing events have been the Korean and Vietnam wars in both their expansion and contraction phases, and the oil, food, and raw materials disturbances of the last few years. However one classifies the last group, they did not reflect instability in the domestic private economy. In addition to these major episodes, government actions have made some other contributions to instability, in the late 1950s and again in 1972–73. Indeed, considering the shocks to which it has been exposed, the private sector has proved remarkably stable. But lest it be thought that I have signed up with Milton Friedman since he won the Nobel Prize, let me hasten to add a few points on the other side. First, the private sector's performance reflects a great many changes in its characteristics that were due to government. A system with a very large government sector, relatively high marginal tax rates, and a large volume of transfer payments including cyclically variable ones like unemployment compensation is inherently far more stable than the small government system ruling before 1929. The spirals generated by any destabilizing event are greatly weakened by the automatic stabilization effect of taxes and transfers. In addition, institutional changes such as deposit insurance have thus far eliminated the financial panics so characteristic of the prewar economy. Moreover, it has always been clear in recession periods that government would intervene before a decline went very far. Antirecession actions have usually been modest in scope and have been slow, but there has been enough action to prevent investors and consumers from panic reactions. Finally, those who feared an overzealous commitment to full employment were wrong. American governments have on the whole been cautious in their peacetime fiscal policies. In peacetime they have seldom taken positive actions that have led to overexpansion. The exception perhaps is the excessive expansion in 1972–73. Nonetheless, the greatest error in the postwar analysis proved to be a failure to apreciate the vulnerability of the U.S. economy and all the market-oriented economies to inflation.

Ever since the mid-1950s a considerable sector of the economics profession has occupied itself with the production and destruction of inflation theories and models. People are usually able to explain the past to their own satisfaction, but each explanation has broken down when tested by its ability to forecast. I will not bore the reader with a play-by-play account of the development and destruction of inflation theories. Instead let me very briefly outline what I think we have learned.

First, it doesn't seem to take very much to start or to accelerate an inflation. As I have already noted, our peacetime economic policies have been fairly cautious, and even in the Korean and Vietnam wars, excess demand has been relatively small. It has never been great enough to produce significant obvious shortages such as we observed during World War II. But we can start an inflation without a great amount of excess demand. When a fairly rapid expansion brings us close to full utilization of resources, we set off a series of price and wage increase in those sectors where resources are most fully utilized and which are most affected by the expansion. As Charles Schultz pointed out 20 years ago, a rapid general expansion is nearly always an unbalanced expansion, with some sectors growing much faster than the overall average. Periods of accelerating inflation have always been periods of rapid expanion of output, and the rate of expansion may be just as important a factor in causing price acceleration as the level of output reached at the peak of the cycle.

Once an inflation has started, it gets built into the system fairly quickly. The initial series of price and wage increases represents a redistribution of income—not just between labor and capital but often between one labor group and another. Even if the economy adjusts to a position that would not in itself produce inflation, with a moderate rate of growth and no widespread labor shortages, the distributional problem is not resolved. The losers who suffered absolute or relative declines in real income are seeking to recoup their losses while the winners are saying, "What have you done for me lately?" If wages rise in response to past price increases and labor cost increases are passed through into price increases, the initial inflationary impulse can generate a wage-price spiral that goes on indefinitely. Because of the lags in the system, it may even accelerate for a time. To reverse the process, one of two things has to happen. When the initial impetus comes from a run-up in raw material and food prices, a sharp decline in those prices may serve to slow down the wage-price spiral. That process played a significant role in halting the Korean War inflation. Alternatively, a sufficiently high rate of unemployment can force workers in the weakest sectors (and with weakest organization) to accept a redistribution of income by taking wage increases that do not compensate for past inflation. But if the level of unemployment is only moderate, that process may take a long time.

The inflation spiral of the late 1950s was broken up by the recessions of 1958 and 1960–61. The Vietnam inflation was probably unwinding, even without the aid of price control, when the inflation was reaccelerated by the 1972–73 boom and the oil and food price inflation. Even with nearly 8 percent unemployment, the United States is making very slow progress in unwinding that episode.

Once an inflation gets started or accelerates to a new level, we have to pay a very heavy price to achieve a significant deceleration. In that connection, it is important to note that the real social cost of inflation is in the process of acceleration. We can live with a significant steady rate of inflation once we are adjusted to it. There is no need to pay a great deal in order to achieve a rapid reduction in the inflation rate.

Another peculiar aspect of the accepted wisdom of the postwar period was the general neglect of supply-side problems by macro-economists. For a set of people bent on using the power of government to stabilize the economy, they were peculiarly sanguine about the ability of the private sector to provide enough capital and raw material supplies in the right places. This laissez-faire attitude reflected the postwar attitudes in which fear of depression outweighed concern for supply problems. It endured for many years because bottlenecks and raw material shortages did not appear for a long time after the Korean War. In fact, the United States went through a raw materials cycle in which the fruits of post-Korean development and exploration and the effects of materials substitution drove down relative prices of raw materials and ultimately retarded development, bringing about a reversal of the relative price cycle in the late 1960s. In agriculture, a burst of technical change and vast investment in farm capital (fostered by price stabilization programs) brought about surpluses that, though burdensome at times, made price stabilization easy. General capital shortages—as opposed to bottlenecks in raw materials processing—have not yet appeared, but there is good reason for concern over aggregate capital supplies in the next four years. I will discuss the capital shortage problem in more detail when I deal with current policy issues later in this essay.

When we turn to our evaluation of policy instruments, we find that most of the conventional wisdom of 30 years ago has been discarded. The use of public works for contracyclical purposes has been regarded as an error for years. They have proved too slow to get started and too expensive to turn off to use for stabilization purposes. That change in view reflects in part the relatively high standards of performance we began to ask for once the system proved more stable than expected. In 1946 no one was hoping for a fine tuning that would eliminate every squiggle on the chart. For big depressions the timing characteristics of public works are unimportant. Indeed we could use some now. In addition, the timing problems of public works apply to the relatively large Corps of Engineer projects involving elaborate engineering studies and land takings. Recent experiments with federal financing of smaller-scale local public works may work better.

Over the years we have come to rely much more heavily on tax rate changes for stabilization purposes. Variations in the personal income tax and the investment credit have been made more speedily than was thought possible until the 1960s. We still have a long way to go, however, before we have a fully effective system of tax adjustments. Moreover, there is still a good deal of controversy over the effectiveness of tax rate changes, especially temporary ones. The 1964 tax reduction received rave reviews from almost everyone, but there has been little agreement since then.

The shifts in accepted views about the relative usefulness of different kinds of fiscal policy instruments are minor compared to the rise and the incipient decline of monetarism. The old monetarism of the simple quantity theory was killed by Keynes and the facts of the 1930s. He provided a theoretical explanation—not by any means the only possible one—for the failure of the predictions of the simple quantity theory to conform to the facts of the 1930s. Milton Friedman, working almost alone for many years, revived the quantity theory with the aid of the experience of the late 1950s and particularly the late 1960s. He has, to use his own expression, used mountains of other evidence, but the convincer for a great many people was the experience of the last two decades and particularly the experience of the late 1960s. A simple line chart shows the crude association between the acceleration of inflation in the late 1960s and the accelerated growth of the money supply. At a more sophisticated level, the staff of the Federal Reserve Bank of St. Louis showed that we could give a fairly good explanation of movements of current GNP up to the late 1960s in terms of a simple moving average of the growth of money supply. Moreover, their equation seemed to show that fiscal policy had little influence. To cap it off, they made a forecast in late 1968 that predicted a more prosperous 1969 than the official forecasters who used a Keynesian approach. They were right. Actually, they overpredicted 1969 GNP by about as much as their rivals underpredicted, but in the circumstances they gained credit for good forecasting. A great deal has happened since then, and I cannot attempt to present a play-by-play account of real events or research events, but I will give my judgment on the outcome. First, the simple St. Louis equation has not worked well since its 1969 success. Nothing has worked very well, but the St. Louis equation has fared worse than other models. Second, revised versions of the St. Louis single-equation approach have accorded much more significance to fiscal policy than the original—without, however, much weakening the effect attributed to monetary policy. Third, models built along Keynesian lines also accord important weight to both monetary and fiscal policy. Thus, there is a convergence of views, which eliminates much of the controversy.

I have given a somewhat bland account of what has happened. Looking at the process from a distance, one is inclined to give the economics profession good marks for scientific objectivity in achieving this resolution. But, looked at close up, the day-by-day process is an adversary proceeding for getting at the truth that bears a good deal of resemblance to Perry Mason reruns, though every economist has his own views as to who is playing Perry Mason and who is Hamilton Burger, the misguided D.A. To conclude that, in choosing among "Money Doesn't Matter," "Money Matters," and "Only Money Matters," the middle one is correct may even seem like plea bargaining.

The conclusions may appear a little less bland if we put them in terms of some issues relevant to policy making. First, it is agreed that if the monetary authorities impose a limit on growth of the money supply, they can limit the rate of inflation even in the face of strongly expansionary fiscal policy or a boom generated by the private sector. On the other hand, there is no assurance that limiting monetary growth will stop inflation very quickly or do so in a smooth way. On the contrary, there are good reasons for believing that monetary resistance to expansionary forces will produce a financial panic.

Second, it is generally agreed that monetary policy influences expenditures through a complex set of linkages. Central bank action impinges directly on short-term interest rates; these in turn influence other security prices, and the liquidity positions of financial institutions; and finally these financial market reactions affect consumers and business expenditures. These reactions are spread out over a long period of time, and their magnitude depends in part on the interaction of monetary policy with other factors and on the initial situation of all the parties involved. Moreover, since prices of assets depend heavily on expectations about the future, the impact of monetary actions depends on investors' beliefs about many aspects of the future including the central bank's intentions.

In the face of those considerations, monetary policy does not look attractive as a precise instrument of stabilization.

To summarize then, we have learned a lot from the experience of the past 30 years, and a good deal of what we have learned is calculated to make life harder for policy makers. Indeed, the one lesson we could agree on is the need for humility. We are not going to be able to control the economy with great precision, and we are likely to continue to walk a tightrope between too much unemployment and too much inflation. We have to face the fact that our policy instruments work with long lags. Given that fact, stabilization policy has to be based on forecasts. Unfortunately, the forecasts are subject to substantial errors. Moreover, the forecasts of the effects of policy changes are subject to especially wide error. Errors of 1 percent in forecasting the average GNP for a calendar year are not uncommon. Errors of 2 percent in the growth rate from the end of one year to the end of the next are not surprising. The errors in forecasts of events more than a year ahead are very wide. When economists tell you that the growth rate for a particular year will be (say) 5 percent, they mean 3 percent to 7 percent, though perhaps most of the time the range will be as little as 4 percent to 6 percent. At the same time, the policies to be chosen now will have effects that will be felt for at least a couple of years ahead.

I need hardly remind the reader, after the experience of the last few years, that failures in stabilization policy in either direction can be costly to our society. Excess unemployment is economically wasteful and has a cancerous effect on our social fabric. Accelerations in the rate of inflation are painful in themselves, and the price of halting them is excessive unemployment. We cannot avoid making some mistakes, but our experience in stabilization policy does suggest some lessons that can be used to minimize errors in either direction.

First, how should policy be related to forecasts? Some people are inclined to take the view that since forecasts are inaccurate, we should always wait to see whether a forecast of a deviation from target levels of output and employment is correct and then take action. That view is, in my judgment, completely wrong. Forecasts may be in error, but they do usually point in the right direction. To wait until a forecasted recession or a forecasted surge of excess demand has actually occurred will force us to take massive action to correct the error. The correction must not only correct for the deviation from the desired position that has already taken place but must also offset the momentum of destabilizing forces in either direction. It may take a long time to restore the economy to a new equilibrium. The alternative is to move promptly in the direction indicated by forecasts but to do so on a modest scale, in effect acting as though one wished to correct the forecasted deviation gradually over a long period. This will result in many small errors and frequent relatively small changes in policy but will avoid the much larger errors involved in a wait-and-see policy. Obviously, however, the appropriate action depends on how far one is from the target growth. If by reason of past errors, we are initially a long distance away, then relatively vigorous action in the expansive or restrictive direction is called for. Even then, however, it has to be recalled that the total effect of any policy action is spread out over a long time. Consequently we must either plan to correct the error rather slowly or take action that will correct the error in a hurry but cause an over-shoot in the other direction and require an abrupt and relatively large-scale reversal of policy. The message is then, that if we are to avoid creating instability in the economy and in the use of policy instruments, we have to take a relatively cautious approach to correction of our economic ills.

It follows from all this that in the area of fiscal policy, we should be seeking to develop procedures that maximize the flexibility of our policy. We should be able to make marginal adjustments in the expenditure budget with some frequency, and we should not require months of debate before making modest changes in tax rates. I shall get away from those generalizations to something more concrete when I examine current fiscal policy issues a little later in this essay.

Finally, for the reasons already presented, monetary policy is very unsatisfactory as an instrument of active stabilization policy. At the same time, there is no basis for choosing the correct long-term growth rate for money supply. Shifts in financial structure such as the development of Negotiable Order of Withdrawal (NOW) accounts make it difficult to give an unambiguous definition of the monetary magnitude whose growth rate is to be fixed.

Nevertheless, monetary policy does have important effects on the economy, and it must have a role in stabilization policy. After wrestling with the problem for a long time, I have come to the conclusion that monetary policy ought to be used as a kind of semi-automatic stabilizer. We ought to operate monetary policy with medium-term goals in mind, choosing a target rate of growth of M_1, or some variant, in a way that seems consistent with a desirable path for nominal income over a period of a couple of years. Since that requires forecasting and forecasts are subject to errors, revisions in the chosen path will be necessary. But it is the essence of a gradualist policy that we make only small-quantity revisions in the chosen path. That means that we accept relatively large short-term variations in short-term interest rates. By doing so, we pay some cost and make some errors. In return, however, the relatively smooth growth of monetary aggregates provides automatic stabilization against unexpected shifts in the real demand or the inflation rate.

After this rather lengthy exposition, I shall try to apply my summary of the lessons of experience to the policy problems facing the Carter administration.

The new administration comes into office in circumstances that present a sharp conflict between short- and long-run objectives of economic policy. The U.S. economy has recovered from the recession that began three years ago, but output has only recently passed the peak reached in late 1973. In effect, the United States has lost three years of normal growth. That loss is reflected in an unemployment rate of nearly 8 percent and in the low level of capacity utilization. Almost everyone agrees that American labor and capital resources should be more fully utilized. Moreover, after a burst of growth in the last half of 1975 and the first part of 1976, the rate of growth of demand has slowed to a pace that is barely high enough to maintain the present level of resource utilization. Most forecasters have assumed that some additional fiscal and/or monetary stimulus will be required to accelerate the growth of demand or even to keep it from decelerating further.

Most economists are prepared to advise the new administration, "Don't just stand there—do something." But there is not so much unanimity on either the amount or the form of the stimulus that should be administered. From a very short-run point of view, it may appear that the United States could use a lot of almost any kind of stimulus. But from a longer-run point of view, every set of program proposals raises conflicts between the immediate objectives and one or another of the potential future problems of the United States.

In choosing an economic stimulus package, the new administration has to decide first on where it wants to go, in terms of its ultimate target for the level of unemployment. Second, it has to decide how fast it wants to get there, and third, it has to choose a mix of policy instruments for achieving those objectives. In all three cases, the conflict between a desire for a low unemployment rate and the fear of a reacceleration of inflation will be its concern.

There appears to be widespread agreement that the United States is going to have to accept a relatively high rate of unemployment if it is to avoid a reacceleration of inflation. Most of the statistical evidence supports the view that inflation will accelerate if the unemployment rate stays below 5.5 percent or so for an extended period. This mark-up from the 4 percent target accepted 30 years ago results from two factors. First, the 4 percent figure was probably too optimistic to begin with. Second, changes in the composition of the labor force have increased the relative numbers of women and young people whose high rates of movement into and out of the labor force lead to higher rates of frictional unemployment.

In choosing its desired path of approach to its unemployment target, the administration has to recognize that U.S experience suggests that the rate of growth of output as well as the level is an important factor in determining the rate of inflation. When the U.S. is anywhere near full utilization of its resources, high rates of growth of output cause bottlenecks and put pressure on prices and wages in particular sectors long before full utilization is reached in the economy as a whole. There is, therefore, a speed limit in the growth rate and it is a limit that gets lower as the nation gets closer to its target rate of utilization.

Finally, in choosing its policies, the administration has to take account of the fact that fiscal and monetary policy influences the composition of output as well as the level and rate of growth. In particular it has to worry about the need for a rise in the rate of capital formation as the nation approaches full employment.

For the reasons given earlier, we cannot expect a demand creation program by itself to reduce unemployment to less than 5.5 percent within, say, the next three to five years. Some special measures may enable the United States to do better, and I shall discuss them later, but in examining the measures that can be taken to increase demand I shall take the 5.5 percent figure as a working target. That implies a reduction of 2.5 percent from the present unemployment rate. An expansion in demand implies not only the employment of more workers but also an increase in the average work week, an increase in the growth of productivity, and a return of discouraged workers to the labor force. GNP must grow an extra 3 percent for every 1-point reduction in the unemployment rate. The United States needs therefore to achieve an extra growth of 7.5 percent on top of the normal 4 percent growth rate that is required to balance normal productivity and labor force growth. That extra growth can of course be spread over a period of several years. To make unemployment fall to 5.5 percent in three years, for example, the United States would need an average growth rate of 6.5 percent per year for three years—4 percent normal growth plus 2.5 percent per year to work off the initial 7.5 percent gap. A four-year program would require an average rate of growth of just under 6 percent.

It is clear that if the United States is to achieve full employment even moderately soon, it must for a time make demand grow at abnormally rapid rates to make up for the slow growth of the past three years. But if it is to reach full employment and not overshoot the mark, the rate of growth ought to modulate downward toward the sustainable growth rate well before the employment target is reached. If the economy reaches full employment at a high rate of growth and we then try restrictive measures to produce a sudden slowdown to normal growth, we take two serious risks: (1) that it takes some time for restrictive measures to work and thus the inflation reaccelerates and (2) that the lagged responses of the economy plunge the nation into recession when the restrictive measures do work. It is almost impossible to change rates of growth of demand quickly enough to produce a quick slowdown at the moment of reaching full employment without producing *both* inflationary pressure and a recession.

That seems to suggest that an optimal program would involve a fast acceleration and a gradual slowdown. For example, consider a path with rates of growth of 8 percent, 6 percent, 5 percent, and 4.5 percent in successive years. That adds up right but poses two problems. First, if achieved, those early very rapid growth rates could very well create some price pressures in some raw materials areas, and if inflationary expectations have any effect on actual inflation, such a rapid expansion would certainly set them off. I would attempt to analyze further the pros and cons of that point, if I thought there were any reliable ways to achieve that kind of path. In fact, it is hard to see how it could be brought off. To do it, we should have to use a ballistic missile approach to fiscal policy. We would have to provide a very large initial stimulus over a short period— say a year—then withdraw the stimulus and let its lagged but waning effects carry the economy forward at a gradually slower pace. The initial stimulus would have to be very large—around $40 billion (in direct expenditure), and we have very little idea of the results. They might give a positive expectational response much larger than the arithmetic of multipliers and accelerators would indicate. On the other hand, cautious reactions to fears of inflation and future tight money might produce a much weaker response. I can only conclude that it is dangerous to use explosives. Finally, there is no way short of a war to start a very large direct expenditure program in a hurry, and the effects of a very large tax reduction would be spread out over a considerable period.

If the United States cannot have a quick burst of growth, it is probably going to have to stretch out the approach to full employment over a period of several years. To avoid bottleneck problems, the United States probably cannot opt for a policy intended to produce growth rates of over, say, 6 percent anywhere in the recovery period. The 1977 rate will of necessity be considerably lower than that and the growth rate must taper off at the end. That implies a rather gradual approach to even a cautiously defined full-employment target.

To complicate it all, we want to end with the right mix of output. To make up for the relatively low rate of capital formation in the last couple of years and to provide extra capital for energy and pollution abatement, the United States will need an unusually high rate of capital formation in the early 1980s.

This large potential demand for capital arises from two sources. First, overall private investment requirements have been increased by the need for special investments to meet pollution abatement and safety requirements. Those investments may be socially valuable, but they are added on top of the investments required for capacity expansion and productivity increase. Additional investment demands are required to meet U.S. energy problems. Finally, the United States must make up the deficit from the relatively low capital formation rates of the last few years.

At the moment, there are no visible signs of capital shortage. Capacity utilization is unusually low in almost all industries; plant and equipment investment has not yet reached the 1973 level and has declined relative to GNP. Investment projections based on surveys indicate that business investment in real terms will increase very little during 1977. Nonetheless, there is widespread agreement that, as the United States approaches full employment, it will be necessary to increase the share of GNP going into capital formation and that private saving may not match the private demand for capital. There is wide variation in the estimates of the possible shortfall, but even the most conservative estimates show a gap between full employment, private savings, and the full-employment demand for investment in the early 1980s. The estimates are based on the assumption that real interest rates and rates of taxation affecting investment do not change much. In principle, the gap can be filled in any one of three ways: (1) excess demand for capital could be removed by a sufficient rise in real interest rates; (2) investment incentives could be reduced by eliminating the investment credit and by other tax measures; and (3) the available savings supply could be increased by running a surplus in the federal budget.

We cannot view the first two solutions with equanimity. They would require a timely application of restrictive measures, and in the field of capital formation, where there are long lags between decisions and actual expenditures, timely means well in advance of the moment when the problem becomes obvious to everyone. If action were delayed too long, the capital goods boom could create general excess demand and new inflationary pressures.

It follows that we ought to be using fiscal policy in ways that are consistent with the achievement of at least a balanced budget and possibly of some surplus in the early 1980s. Revenues will be growing as the economy expands, but existing program commitments will absorb most of that additional income. A number of budget projections indicate that if the budget is to be in balance when the United States reaches 5.5 percent unemployment, the government cannot make any substantial permanent tax reduction or adopt substantial permanent expenditure programs before about 1982.

All these considerations severely limit the options of the new administration. In fact they provide, it seems to me, the basic framework for the kind of policy proposed by the administration. If long-term considerations preclude the adoption of permanent tax reductions or large expanding permanent expenditure programs, the only expansionary options left are temporary tax cuts and expenditure programs of the public service job and local public works type. The efficacy of temporary tax reductions may be debated. It may take a couple of dollars of temporary tax reduction to produce the expenditure effect of $1 of permanent cut, but if I am right about the capital formation problem, there is no real choice.

The administration program does include some permanent tax reduction, and that uses up some of the small amount of budget leeway available. Consistency requires that the administration resist new expenditure programs vigorously. The one thing that seems to be lacking in the administration program is investment stimulus. Capital formation this year or next year will reduce the need for capital formation in the future as well as create needed demand now. A good case can be made for a fairly large temporary increase in the investment credit.

Given the uncertainties of forecasting, we have no assurance that the administration's program will work out as planned. Its success depends in part on the notion that a general expansion of demand will stimulate plant and equipment investment so that the private-sector expansion replaces the waning stimulus from temporary tax reductions and expenditure programs. Even if that works out, we are still exposed to uncertainties about the rate of inflation. After a sharp deceleration from the peak rates of inflation in 1974–75, the rate of inflation seems to have leveled off at 5–6 percent per year. Further progress is uncertain, and there is certainly a serious risk that sharp increases in food, raw material, or energy prices will trip off a new acceleration. Indeed, it is the fear of accelerating inflation rather than the need to drive the inflation rate to zero that makes us cautious about demand expansion.

Finally, even if the administration's program worked out in terms of both employment and inflation, a 5.5 percent unemployment rate is nothing to write home about. Arthur Okun once suggested that the economic discomfort index could be defined as the sum of the unemployment and inflation rates. A discomfort index of 11—5.5 each from unemployment and inflation sounds a little blank to me. Is there anything we can do to make things a little more comfortable?

Actually there are a lot of possibilities, but each of them has its own difficulties. I shall close by merely mentioning a few broad categories. First, we can continue to improve our fiscal policy. We have made considerable progress in bringing Congress effectively into the budgetary process and in putting budget making into a longer-run framework. If Congress can work effectively in that area, we may also be able to get greater flexibility into tax policy, particularly in the investment area. Second, the conflict between price stability and unemployment can be reduced by better and more flexible manpower training programs. This country began those programs 15 years ago. Their successes have been modest indeed. Nonetheless, if pursued patiently and realistically, they could lead to reductions in unemployment without any inflationary cost.

Third, there are many possibilities though no panacea for stabilizing food and raw material prices and thereby reducing inflationary pressures. Finally, we have long been aware that government contributes to inflation through regulatory and other anticompetitive policies. Changes in those areas could in the long run contribute significantly to the reduction of inflationary pressure.

All of these areas are relatively unexplored. We have learned a lot from our past experience. I am hopeful that we are applying some of what we have learned, but it's clear that we still have a lot to learn.

6

THE SEARCH FOR THE GRAIL: ECONOMIC POLICY ISSUES OF THE LATE 1970s

Marina v. N. Whitman

Regarding the title of this essay, some may feel that all this should really be taking place in church on Sunday morning. So perhaps I should begin by explaining why I have responded to a query about what advice I, as a former member of the Council of Economic Advisers, would give the president today with a discussion of "The Search for the Grail." The Holy Grail was the cup from which Christ had drunk at the Last Supper and which, according to legend, would bring eternal bliss to anyone who managed to find and capture it. And so, one bonny knight after the other set out in search of this miraculous cup. The problem was that, whenever anyone came near and tried to snatch it, it receded, and hung in the air, eternally just out of reach.

It seems to me that the problems of political economy confronting the president of the United States or, indeed, the head of state of any other large industrialized country, are like the Holy Grail in one very important respect—that is, the kinds of economic goals that modern governments have set for themselves, or had thrust upon them by their electorates, can never be fully realized. As we seem to get closer to the goal, it moves tantalizingly just out of reach.

I will cast my discussion in terms of what I think are the major economic problems the president faces at this particular time. I don't think they would be very different if he were at the helm of any of the other leading industrialized countries. The centerpiece of the problem is what, in recent years, we have come to call stagflation. The awkwardness of the word reflects the awkwardness of a situation for which there are no textbook answers. Most introductory economic textbooks have a chapter, or at least part of one, that presents a clear-cut prescription for government behavior when confronted with domestic recession or depression. The monetary authorities should expand the money supply more rapidly than usual, and those in charge of taxing and spending should shift fiscal policy in a stimulative direction, expanding the government deficit (or reducing the surplus) by cutting taxes, increasing public spending, or both. Contemporary textbooks are equally clear about the prescription when inflation is the problem: Do exactly the opposite, tighten up on the growth of the money supply and reduce the deficit in the government budget (or increase the surplus) by increasing taxes and/or cutting down government spending. The only thing that the textbooks don't tell you is what to do when you are confronted with both problems at the same time. And that, unfortunately, is the situation we are confronted with, here in the United States and in many other countries as well. It is because of the double-barreled nature of the problem that there is so much disagreement and uncertainty at the moment about what course should be steered by stabilization policy.

This controversy intensified just before the 1976 presidential election and is still going on. How much economic stimulus is appropriate in the current situation, or, indeed, is any additional government stimulus necessary or desirable at all? There is a wide range of disagreement among reasonable and honest people on this question. How one answers it depends partly on one's diagnosis of what caused the problem in the first place—that is, why we have had unprecedentedly high rates of inflation persisting right through a severe recession and continuing to coexist with a high level of unemployment.

One school of thought argues that this phenomenon is a form of expectational hangover from the last boom period, the explosive demand-push inflation of a few years ago. The argument is that this kind of experience builds inflationary expectations, and therefore inflationary behavior, into the warp and woof of the economic system. Once that happens, it takes a long time to squeeze such expectations, and the patterns of behavior they produce, out of the system. Thus, higher rates of inflation may persist, even in the face of substantial unemployment.

The competing view maintains that the high rates of inflation we have been subjected to during the past few years were caused primarily by extraordinary developments on the cost side. The most dramatic of these events was the series of massive increases in the prices of petroleum products engineered by the Organization of Petroleum Exporting Countries (OPEC), but crop failures and shortfalls in various parts of the world also played a significant role, along with some other scattered bits of global bad luck. It is the impact of these phenomena, working its way through wages and prices throughout the economy, that have made high rates of inflation so stubbornly persistent, in this alternative view.

These competing explanations of what has caused the current staflation generate very different prescriptions for the conduct of macroeconomic policy during the current stage of recovery. On the one hand acceptance of the expectational hypothesis suggests a cautious and gradual approach to recovery. If people's expectations are highly inflation-sensitive, the danger is omnipresent that price rises might reaccelerate well before the economy gets up to full employment. Furthermore, in this view, the only way to get the rate of inflation down to normal levels, by historical standards, is to squeeze inflationary expectations out of the economy, a necessarily long and painful process. Many of those who argue that no additional stimulus is needed at present are thinking along these lines.

The alternative approach, which explains the unusually high inflation rates of recent years primarily in terms of nonrecurring cost-push factors, implies that there is little or no danger of reaccelerating inflation under conditions of high unemployment and substantial excess capacity. Thus, the proponents of this view argue, the government should be more aggressive in stimulating the economy than it has been so far.

Added to this divergence of opinion on the causes of stagflation is considerable disagreement about just where the economy stands at the present time. What, for example, is the real meaning of the capacity utilization figures that purport to tell us that we have nearly 20 percent excess capacity at the moment? How much of the capacity that is counted as "excess" in present statistics is really obsolete and uneconomical? There is a general consensus that the economy will encounter severe inflationary pressure long before 100 percent capacity utilization is achieved. In fact, by the most commonly used measure, that level has never been reached. But the serious question is, Do we start getting significant inflationary pressure at 90 percent utilization, or at 85 percent, or even earlier? And what about situations in which the average utilization level is quite low, but there are bottlenecks in particular basic industries? All of these unanswered questions lead to wide disparities in interpretations of where we stand right now and, therefore, in advice regarding the best posture for stabilization policy.

Even more important are widely different views regarding the real meaning of the unemployment data. First of all, economists have a wide range of opinions on what the "full-employment unemployment view" is today. Most of them agree that for many reasons, particularly the greatly increased share of the total accounted for by women and teenagers who are new entrants to the work force, that rate is no longer the 4 percent that was enshrined throughout much of the postwar period. The outgoing Council of Economic Advisers wrote in its January 1977 report that the full-employment unemployment rate is probably between 4.9 and 5.5 percent. Some other economists think it is even higher; one recent study suggests an estimate of over 6 percent. Wherever the exact truth lies, it is clear that the magical full-employment level of unemployment is higher than we used to think—and higher than many still think. At the same time, it is clear that the unemployment rates of 1976 and early 1977—between 7 and 8 percent—are significantly above the full-employment level.

In addition to questions about what a given level of unemployment means in terms of excess productive capacity, there is a great deal of disagreement about what a given aggregate level of unemployment implies for human welfare. Is it associated with welfare costs as high as it would have been 30 years ago, when unemployment and welfare benefits were far less available and the number of workers per family was fewer? Should we take account in our welfare judgments of the fact that women and teenagers are a far larger proportion of the labor force than they used to be, and, if so, how? Is it meaningful to lump into one aggregate number the unemployed head of a household—man or woman—and the unemployed high school student living at home and seeking a job that will fit his school schedule? On the other hand, should we really exclude from the unemployment figures the so-called discouraged workers—people who are no longer looking for jobs, not because they don't want one or need one, but because they have become convinced that they won't be able to find one? The answers different people give to such questions as these have a lot to do with how they evaluate the nature and the urgency of the unemployment problem.

There is another anomaly that further confuses the issue: While the unemployment rate is today extremely high by historical standards, the employment rate (the proportion of the population aged 16 or over that is employed) is also at an historically high level. Measured in terms of the unemployment rate, the most recent recession was by far the most severe one this country has experienced since the 1930s. Yet, in contrast with some earlier recessions, the total number of people employed dropped very little during this most recent one, and the employment ratio remained above the level of that in most other postwar recessions (see the following table). The explanation of this paradox is, of course, that the labor-force participation rate has been increasing. But that still leaves us with the question of what conclusions to draw. Should we look at the unemployment rate and conclude that the situation is very bad and improving much too slowly to be acceptable? Or should we look at the employment rate and argue that, by historical standards, things are really not so bad at all? There is ample room for disagreement here.

Employment and Unemployment in
Recession Years
(in percent)

Business Cycle Low (1)	Unemployment Rate (2)	Employment Ratio (3)
1949	5.9	54.6
1954	5.5	53.8
1958	6.8	54.2
1961	6.7	54.2
1970	4.9	56.1
1975	8.5	55.3

Sources: Column (1): Business-cycle trough years, National Bureau of Economic Research, Inc.; column (2): Unemployment as percentage of civilian labor force, U.S. Bureau of Labor Statistics; and column (3): Civilian employment as percentage of population 16 years old and over, U.S. Bureau of Labor Statistics. Table taken from Geoffrey H. Moore, "Unemployment, and the Inflation-Recession Dilemma," in *Contemporary Economic Problems*, ed. William Fellner (Washington, D.C.: American Enterprise Institute, 1976).

Even if there were no uncertainty and disagreement about what caused the present stagflation or about the implications of current data on unemployment and capacity utilization, we would still be confronted with the practical problem of how best to alleviate the unemployment situation. The policy alternatives available can be categorized in a number of different ways. But one fundamental difference is between direct and indirect job creation. The government can either undertake direct job creation itself, in the form of public service or public works programs, or it can give direct subsidies to employment in the private sector. The alternative approach is via policies that stimulate investment in the private sector, increasing the size of productive capacity and, thus, of employment opportunities. Many people argue that this second approach—which one noted labor leader has derisively termed the "trickle-down" approach—is too slow and too unreliable to be effective when the nation is confronted with an acute unemployment problem.

I think it's probably true that the direct job-creation approach is likely to produce faster results than the investment stimulus, although even that is not entirely certain. The other side of the coin is the differing implications of the two approaches for the growth of labor productivity and therefore of real wages—that is, not the dollar amount of a worker's weekly paycheck, but its purchasing power in terms of the goods and services it can buy. Because, although in the short run it is possible to increase the worker's purchasing power by somehow giving labor a larger share of total output, and other factors of production a correspondingly smaller share, in the long run there has to be a fairly close relationship between the rate at which labor productivity grows and the rate at which real wages increase.

The problem with relying primarily on direct job creation is that if we simply create more jobs, without simultaneously creating more capital through investment, labor productivity will decline or, at best (if better technology is being introduced), fail to rise as fast as it would have otherwise. To the extent that jobs are created by stimulating investment and, thus, net capital formation and output capacity, labor productivity will be enhanced.

To nobody's surprise, I'm sure, the policies that are actually being proposed and debated today are various compromise packages among the alternatives I have just described. President Carter's stimulus proposals, as finally modified and implemented by the Congress, are likely to involve something of each—some public job programs and direct subsidy to wages (perhaps in the form of a credit on the employer's share of social security taxes), and some stimulus to investment in the form of reduced corporate taxes or an increased investment tax credit, or perhaps the elimination of double taxation on dividends. In fact, one early Carter proposal offered private business a choice: firms could select to receive either an increase in their investment tax credit or a direct subsidy to increased employment in the form of a reduction in their social security contribution for new employees. I suspect that it is because of the underlying trade-off between speed and certainty on the one hand and the impact on productivity and real wages on the other that Americans are being offered a potpourri, a little bit of this and a little bit of that.

The form in which employment stimulus is provided—public works or public service jobs as against incentives to the private sector—also affects the allocation of total output between the public and the private sectors of the economy. Differences in view on this point involve a Friedman-versus-Galbraith argument over whether economic welfare is better served by increased consumption of private goods, purchased in the marketplace, or by increased consumption of public goods, acquired through the political process of taxing and spending.

Slicing the problem another way, we face the question of whether we should rely primarily, or even exclusively, on overall economic stimulus to reduce unemployment, trusting that, as President Kennedy once remarked, "a rising tide lifts all boats," even those most deeply mired in unemployment. The problem is that an infusion of economic stimulus massive enough to reduce the unemployment of such high-unemployment groups as black teenagers to desirable levels would very probably push the economy into a situation of bottlenecks and serious inflationary pressure. Thus, many people feel that the government should be devoting more attention to policies and programs selectively targeted on those groups that experience chronically high unemployment rates. The programs of this type that have been tried in this country in recent years have not been terribly encouraging. But some European countries that have experimented with such programs far more extensively than has the United States have apparently had more success. At present, the question of the relative importance that should be assigned to general stimulus on the one hand and specialized employment programs on the other remains both uncertain and controversial.

Closely related to the problem of stagflation and unemployment reduction is that of capital shortage. This whole issue is a complex one, and, at least initially, it was presented in a very confusing way. Discussions of an impending capital shortage seemed to be based on the notion that there is a necessary one-to-one relationship between the rate of investment and the growth rate of employment. Assuming that this relationship holds, projecting the growth rate of the labor force out over the next decade or so, and then adding in the increased investment that will be required for purposes—such as environmental control or energy conservation—that do not expand output capacity, produces a required rate of investment that is very high by historical standards in this country (although not necessarily by the standards of other industrialized countries, nearly all of which invest a larger proportion of gross national product than does the United States). The results of these exercises indicate that the rate of investment required to maintain high employment will be difficult to reach, and that it will be achievable only if this nation managed to sustain a prolonged surplus in the budget of the federal government, which, on the basis of past experience, does not seem very probably, to say the least.

The trouble with this approach is that is assumes fixed capital-output ratios—that is, a very rigid economy unable to alter either the mix of goods and services it turns out or the production processes it uses to produce them. This kind of argument is frequently made with regard to the economies of certain less-developed countries, but it seems to be a peculiar one to apply to a large advanced economy like the United States. In fact, we could in principle achieve a particular growth rate of employment with many different rates of investment. But it would involve different capital-output ratios—that is, different methods of production, as well as a different mix of goods and services produced. Specifically, for employment to grow more rapidly than the rate of capacity-increasing investment, the amount of capital available per worker would have to drop. All other things being equal, this would reduce the growth rate of labor productivity and, therefore, of real wages. Thus, the real "capital shortage" issue is not simply whether we can provide enough work for a growing labor force but whether we can provide it under conditions that also permit an acceptable rate of increase in real wages.

The whole issue is confused further by the fact that, at the present moment, a capital shortage is nowhere to be found. It is true that the rate of investment in the United States is low at the moment, not only in comparison with those of other major countries but also as compared to past U.S. experience, and the capital-goods sector has been weaker than usual so far during this recovery. But this is not due to a capital shortage in the sense of any financial stringency. In fact, all the major groups in the economy are highly liquid just now: Individual savings are high, business balance sheets show a high degree of liquidity, and most banks are actively looking for qualified borrowers to expand their domestic loan portfolios. Wherever we look, there are no signs of the sort of liquidity shortage that might be expected to underlie the low rate of real capital formation. This is a puzzling phenomenon and one that contributes to the general confusion and disagreement regarding the reasons for the present **weakness of investment and the capital-goods sector.**

The explanations offered can be divided into two groups, with widely differing implications for policy. On one side are arguments stressing the long-term decline in the real rate of return on capital suggested by several recent empirical studies, along with the increased risk associated with investment due in part to the climate of uncertainty created by government itself. This line of reasoning suggests that what is needed to increase the rate of investment are government policies that will increase real profit rates, reduce the uncertainties created by government regulatory processes, and shift the thrust of fiscal policy from encouraging consumption toward encouraging investment—that is, generally tip taxing-spending decisions and regulation-deregulation decisions in the direction of giving greater incentives to investment. Among the moves suggested under this rubric are an increase in the investment tax credit, reduction of corporate tax rates, elimination of double taxation of dividends, relaxation of certain environmental standards, and so forth.

A competing explanation concurs that investment is low because the expected rate of return, taking risk factors into account, is low but offers very different reasons. The main factor discouraging investment in new capacity, in this view, is underutilization of existing capacity. There is excess capacity in the United States at the present time, although no one is sure just how much, and this country has just been through the most severe economic downturn since the Great Depression of the 1930s. Businessmen are still insecure about whether demand will grow rapidly and steadily enough to justify their investment in increased capacity. The proponents of this view argue that there are ample savings, plenty of finance available for investment, but that what is missing is the assurance of a high and steady real growth rate to provide assured markets for increased output.

This line of reasoning generates a very different set of policy implications. Here, the stress is on the use of macroeconomic policies and government transfer programs to provide steady growth of demand and assure income maintenance over the business cycle. To achieve these objectives, the government should utilize and continuously refine all the stabilization tools it has at its command. If the government can "fine-tune" successfully, it is argued, that will provide an environment conducive to greater investment.

Thus, even among those who agree that a higher rate of investment is essential in the United States, there is substantial disagreement about what type of policies will most effectively stimulate such investment. All this is reminiscent of the argument three or four decades ago, which occupied some of the best economic minds of the time, over whether the expected long-term economic stagnation of the Western world was attributable to undersaving or to underconsumption. It looks as if we have come full circle, back to this argument once again.

The fourth major issue confronting the policy makers in Washington is the question of allocation of output. What proportion of output in the United States should take the form of private goods, bought and sold in the marketplace and consumed individually, and what proportion should be public goods, allocated through the political process and consumed collectively or not at all? Many people in this country are worried by what they see as the inexorable encroachment of government on an ever increasing share of total output, and insist that what is needed is to cut both taxes and government spending. Others, believing with John Kenneth Galbraith that Americans live in "private affluence and public squalor," insist that this country can rectify the situation only by increasing the share of the public sector, raising taxes as necessary to support increased expenditures.

A brief look at the actual figures reveals that between the end of the Korean War in 1952 and the present, the share of GNP represented by the federal government's purchases of goods and services has fluctuated a certain amount but has shown no trend, either up or down. It was about 22 percent of GNP in 1952, and it is about the same today. However, the share of transfer payments, including social security, unemployment compensation, and welfare programs, has increased substantially. So has the share accounted for by the spending of state and local governments. If we add all these categories together, being careful to avoid double counting, we find that the share of total government expenditures in GNP has risen from about one-quarter of GNP in 1952 to about one-third today. So, as usual, both sides can find numbers to support their particular view of the issue.

A different approach to the question of whether the government's budget should be restored to balance at a high level or a low one, by increasing taxes or reducing expenditures, has to do with whether our main focus is on the demand or the supply side of the economic equation. The Keynesian tradition, the heritage of most English-speaking economists of the postwar era, holds that modern industrialized economies generally operate below the level where supply constraints would become effective, and that economic prosperity therefore depends on policies that ensure the stabilization and growth of aggregate demand. **Supply growth, in this view, is exogenous, depending on factors beyond our control.**

The shortages and inflationary explosions of the past few years have, however, rekindled interest in the supply side, and particularly in the impact that various government policies have on the supply of various factors of production. For instance, a great deal of work has been done recently on the impact of unemployment insurance on the length of time people remain unemployed—that is, on the supply of labor. Of course, unemployment insurance also has an important impact on the demand side, by helping to stabilize family purchasing power over the business cycle. But the major focus right now, the issue on which lots of bright young people are publishing articles in major journals, is on questions of supply. This does not mean that we have returned to a neoclassical world, in which the growth rate is determined exclusively by the growth of factor supplies and demand remains automatically and continuously at the full-employment level. Rather, academic scholars and government advisers and policy makers are beginning to take a more balanced view, looking at both the demand effects and the supply effects of particular government policies.

From the point of view of aggregate demand, it matters little whether the government chooses to exert stimulus by reducing taxes or increasing expenditures (assuming, of course, that it takes the balanced-budget multiplier into account in deciding on the exact magnitude that would make the two alternatives equivalent in impact). Either the government spends the money directly or it leaves more money in the pockets of the taxpayers, who will presumably spend it themselves, although in this latter case there is always some uncertainty about how fast they will spend it, and exactly how much they will decide to tuck away in the bank.

Some economists are beginning to argue, though, that whether the government cuts taxes or increases expenditures makes a significant difference for employment and unemployment from the supply side.

Basically, they argue that by cutting taxes, and thus reducing the "wedge" or discrepancy between the cost of labor to the employer and the amount the worker actually takes home in his pocket, the government will encourage greater expansion of employment than would be achieved by an equivalent increase in public spending.

In its extreme form, this argument is beset with a number of problems, such as the low or zero value it implicitly attaches to public goods. But it does focus attention on an issue worthy of serious consideration. Another aspect of that same general issue is the question of how strong the fiscal bootstraps really are. That is, when the government utilizes fiscal policy to stimulate the economy, to what extent will the increased spending (or reduced taxes) generate additional tax revenues through faster income growth and thereby avoid increasing the budget deficit over the long run? To what extent and under what conditions will the additional government borrowing associated with a larger deficit "crowd out" private borrowing and investment by pushing up interest rates, thus reducing the stimulative impact? More generally, when and under what cirumstances can we expect the long-awaited and so far elusive "fiscal dividend" to materialize, which would permit the government to reduce or eliminate its budget deficit, when such action is appropriate to the current state of the business cycle, without doing violence to ongoing and high-priority new programs?

I was interested to note that, in its most recent analysis, the Congressional Budget Office suggested that, given the administration's current proposals, the only way there could be a surplus in the federal budget by 1980 would be for the economy to grow, in real terms, at an average annual rate of 5 percent, which is extremely high by historical standards. This evaluation raises a serious question about whether the administration's target of a balanced budget by 1980 or 1981 is compatible with the new programs it is offering. And yet, as I stated above, unless we are able to generate federal budget surpluses when aggregate demand conditions warrant them, we are not likely to be able to generate sufficient investment and capital formation to maintain high employment and acceptable real wage growth.

Closely tied in with the question of the allocation of output between the public and the private sectors is another issue that has been receiving a good deal of publicity lately: that of planning. Up until a few years ago, planning was something of a dirty word in this country, politically speaking. Today there is a Commission for National Planning, whose membership includes such unusual bedfellows as Senator Hubert Humphrey, Nobel laureate economist Wassily Leontief, Leonard Woodcock of the United Auto Workers (UAW), and Henry Ford II.

There is a lot of confusion and disagreement, of course, over what is meant by the term "planning." At one extreme are those who argue that it means simply better government information, better statistics, and better coordination of government policies among the various branches of the executive branch, as well as between the executive and legislative branches. Certainly, there are plenty of examples of the government's undoing with its left hand what it is trying to do with its right. Back in the spring and summer of 1973, when I was still a member of the CEA, the most urgent domestic problem we faced was the very rapid increase in food prices, particularly meat prices, that was going on at the time. We were all running around seven days a week like the proverbial chickens with their heads cut off, trying to find ways to reduce the rate of food price inflation. One day, at one of the frequent meetings of the Cost of Living Council (CLC), someone passed around an advisory bulletin that had just been issued by the Department of Agriculture, urging farmers to reduce chicken production by 20 percent in order to forestall a price decline. I don't think I've ever seen anyone angrier than the director of the CLC. A procedure was set up whereby the CLC staff would monitor the Department of Agriculture's marketing orders and advisory bulletins for their potential inflationary impact. But that certainly didn't solve the coordination problems of the federal government.

There is not likely to be much opposition to the idea of having better government coordination, better information, better statistics, although how much we are willing to pay for the latter could be a genuine issue. But there is another and quite different view that sees planning as an expansion of government activity, an increased role for the government in setting investment priorities, whether through the use of selective credit allocation or via some other form of tax, subsidy, or regulation.

I suspect the reason that this view of planning has attracted more attention recently is that the U.S. economy has been subject to a series of shocks in recent years. These shocks were as unpleasant as they were unexpected, and they subjected most Americans to varying degrees of hardship. It is not surprising, therefore, that there is a general feeling that the United States should in the future be better prepared and less vulnerable than it has been in the recent past. That certainly is a reasonable goal. The only problem is that I see very little evidence to suggest that the government would be likely to do a better job than the private sector of foreseeing and forestalling future problems. As I look back at what the government energy policy was just before the OPEC shocks erupted in 1973—or rather, what U.S. petroleum policies were, because it didn't really have anything called an "energy policy" back then—it certainly doesn't seem to me that the government's policies were any more effective in preparing the United States for the "oil shock" than was the behavior of the private sector—neither one of them gets very high marks, to put it mildly.

I think the real need is not for more planning in the sense of a wider scope for government activity, but for us to find ways to reduce the vulnerability of the U.S. economy by introducing a higher degree of what might be called technological pluralism. That is, the United States tends to put very heavy emphasis on doing things in the most efficient way, the least costly way. Most of the changes in U.S. farm policy during the 1970s, for example, were focused on increasing economic efficiency and reducing costs to the taxpayer. That's excellent, all other things being equal, but they aren't always equal. More specifically, we must pay attention also to the degree of vulnerability associated with different policy options. We must be careful not to institute mechanisms and systems that are extremely efficient under one particular set of circumstances, but where costs rise very rapidly if circumstances change and the unexpected occurs. Successful private firms have always, without describing it in those terms, "bought insurance" against uncertainty by setting up their plants and production processes, not necessarily in the form that would be most efficient under one particular most probable set of circumstances, but in a form that would function with a reasonable degree of efficiency under a considerable variety of circumstances. However, when it comes to governmental decision making, with all the emphasis that is placed today on openness and accountability, it may be difficult to operate this way unless there is some public consensus about how we should make the trade-off between efficiency and cost reduction on the one hand and reduced vulnerability on the other. I think that it is this question of response to uncertainty, rather than the issue of more or less government involvement in "planning" as such, that is at the heart of the present concerns of economists.

The final item on my list of the major economic issues facing the president and his advisers has to do with U.S. response to the changing nature of international interdependence. It has become a cliche by now to point out that, with the rapid growth of international trade and investment since the end of World War II, economic interdependence among nations has increased. What is more surprising is that only relatively recently have Americans come to recognize that interdependence is a two-way proposition. There is an old saying, "When the United States sneezes, Europe gets pneumonia." Developments in the United States, in other words, were seen as having a tremendous impact on economic conditions in the rest of the world. But the United States was regarded—and Americans regarded themselves—as too large and too rich and too self-sufficient to be much affected by what went on, economically speaking, in the world outside.

Today, that American self-perception has changed dramatically—

even more sharply, it seems to me, than the change in reality that underlies it. And, having seen the impact that developments abroad—the formation of a petroleum-producers' cartel, crop failures in foreign countries, even changes in the habits of Peruvian anchovies—can have on employment, prices, production, and the level of economic activity in the United States, Americans are stressing the negative aspects of interdependence far more than they used to. Interdependence has always, of course, had two faces. On the one hand, the growth of international trade and investment gave rise to increased specialization, increased efficiency, and faster growth of output and income and standards of living for the world as a whole. On the other hand, interdependence increases the vulnerability of each country to policies and developments outside its own borders, over which it has no control. And this greater vulnerability tends to make governments nervous, particularly in the face of broadened responsibilities for the domestic economy that the governments of the industrialized democracies have taken upon themselves—or had thrust upon them by their electorates—in the postwar era. Thus, there is an inevitable tension between increasing international integration of markets and the demand for national autonomy at the level of economic policy.

Having long focused on the efficiency aspects of economic integration, Americans are now much more aware, in fact probably excessively aware, of the vulnerability aspects. There are many reasons for this. One is the decline of American hegemony in the international economy. The reasons for this are partly political: In the days of the cold war, American economic leadership was accepted as a byproduct or a quid pro quo for the nuclear security blanket that it spread over the noncommunist world; with the diffusion of cold war concerns, there is increasing impatience, both in the United States and abroad, with the special economic role of America. The reasons are partly economic as well: Although the United States remains the world's largest single economy, its shares of the world totals of gross national product, industrial production, exports, and international reserves have all been declining over the postwar period.

Second, the United States, although still the least open economy in the noncommunist world, is a good deal more open than it used to be. The share of foreign trade in the U.S. GNP has virtually doubled in the past few years, the proportion of total profits of U.S. corporations earned abroad has increased substantially, and the United States is dependent on imports for a growing share of its total consumption of a number of basic industrial raw materials. At the same time, we are witnessing a breakdown of the American-led postwar institutional structure surrounding international economic relationships. The Bretton Woods institutions—the International Monetary Fund (IMF), the General Agreement on

Tariffs and Trade (GATT), and, to a lesser, extent, the World Bank—are in a state of upheaval and transition. International aid is a much more complex proposition than it used to be, and American relations with the developing nations are far more complicated and difficult than they appeared 20 years ago. Finally, the United States is confronted with the rediscovery of economic scarcity and the new power of the commodity producers: A new group of countries has suddenly exploded into prominence with an economic and political clout that no one, including they, ever realized they possessed. In sum, the whole framework of the international economic system is in a state of uncertainty and flux.

There are a number of ways in which the United States can respond to this perception of increased vulnerability, of interdependence as a two-way proposition. One would be to create a fortress economy: to cut as many economic ties as possible with the outside world and abdicate any sense of responsibility for global economic leadership. A second would be to undertake a massive economic power play; for example, to counter the OPEC cartel with a North American wheat cartel. It seems to me that neither economic isolation nor the institutionalization of "might makes right" via huge bilateral monopolies is an acceptable alternative. The third alternative is for the United States to continue to play a crucial role in the collective leadership of the international economy, a leadership based no longer on dominance but on persuasion and compromise. This will be a difficult and often frustrating role, but, it seems to me, an essential one for the United States to undertake.

All of the questions I have raised in this essay can be summed up in two very large issues that confront this country and this administration. The first is the issue of the governability of democracies. Can one combine rational economic policy making with the rising economic expectations of every group in society in a political environment in which the government has to deliver or go down at the polls? Or, to put the question another way, can the United States avoid destroying itself by continuously trying to divide up 110 percent of the available pie? Those who believe the answer is yes point to Great Britain and Italy and suggest that the United States is next. I myself am an optimist on this point; not only do I think the United States can avoid falling into such a no-win situation, accompanied by chronic inflation, but I even think the two countries so often used as horrible examples have a decent chance to pull out of their current difficulties. But this question about the compatibility of economic rationality and stability with modern political democracy is a genuine one, not to be taken lightly. My personal answer is yes, it can be done, but it is one of the major challenges faced by this or any administration.

The second overarching issue concerns the survival of a liberal international economic system. Until relatively recently the framework for international trading, investment, and monetary relationships was based on a general, if unarticulated consensus: It was taken for granted that the ultimate goal of the system was to maximize world efficiency and international harmony by minimizing the distortions and uncertainty created by the existence of national boundaries. That is, the system was laissez-faire in its orientation and neutral in its intent. That is not to deny that each of the participants in the system practiced, in varying degrees, interventionist or restrictive policies vis-a-vis particular aspects of their own economies, and the system proved relatively flexible in accommodating the international ramifications of these policies. Nor did the goal of neutrality prevent wrangles over whose interests the system was serving and efforts to modify its operation in favor of one nation (or group of nations) or another. But the liberal thrust of the system was nonetheless clear and generally accepted.

Today, these fundamental principles of the international system are under serious challenge. Over the postwar period, the domestic economic goals of most industrialized nations have broadened from a primary focus on efficiency and growth to an intensified concern with economic and social stability and distributional equity. The political importance of these concerns, together with the increased vulnerability that is one face of interdependence, sets up countervailing pressures against a laissez-faire international framework directed toward promoting market integration. An even more urgent challenge arises from the increasing prominence and activism of a relatively new group of participants in the international system: the developing countries. Despite their political, cultural, social, and economic heterogeneity, most of these nations share a common belief that the "neutrality" of the postwar international economic system has operated to their disadvantage and are firm in their insistence on the construction of a "New International Economic Order" that takes the international redistribution of income as an explicit and primary goal. Is it possible to fashion an international economic system that can incorporate these emergent goals and participants and reconcile them with a basically liberal thrust? This is an urgent question and one on which the United States, as the leading modern proponent of economic liberalism, must carry a major share of the responsibility.

And now, at last, for a bit of advice to my successors in those elegant CEA offices in the Old Executive Office Building next to the White House. Although my own views and biases have surfaced frequently, I suspect, in the preceding discussion, I am not going to close with a list of explicit policy recommendations on each of the issues I have raised here. If I tried, given my propensity for "on the other hand" qualifications (I am reminded of Harry Truman's fervent plea, "Dear God, give me a one-handed economist"), this essay could turn into a book. Rather, let me wind up with a few general thoughts for all seasons.

The first bit of general advice is, Don't get mesmerized by the numbers. The business of the CEA is numbers, of course, to collect the very best data that are available, analyze them, interpret their essential significance for the president, make forecasts based on them, and use them as the basis for generating policy analyses and, ultimately, policy recommendations. Because of this preoccupation with quantitative information, which is the economist's stock in trade, it is easy to fall prey to the temptation to confuse the data with the reality they imperfectly summarize and represent, and to substitute measures aimed at improving the indexes for measures designed to alleviate the underlying problem. And they are not always the same, by any means. It would be easy to eliminate the rise in the Consumer Price Index, for example, by imposing a universal price freeze, or to reduce the unemployment rate by eliminating all unemployment compensation, drafting all young people between the ages of 16 and 19 into military service or a Civilian Conservation Corps, or forbidding all married women with employed husbands from seeking jobs. But such policies would not improve the general welfare; indeed, they would drastically reduce it. These are extreme examples, of course, and no one is seriously suggesting them. But they serve to underline the difference between fixing the numbers and dealing with the underlying problem. I have little patience, on the other hand, with people who say, "Oh, the statistics don't mean anything, they certainly don't reflect *my* experience at the supermarket or in job hunting." The aggregate data collected and published by the U.S. government are produced honestly, they reflect the most sophisticated statistical techniques available, they are better than the statistics of any other nation, and they give us information about the state of the U.S. economy that we couldn't possibly get otherwise. They are an invaluable servant of the president and his advisers in economic policy making; the only danger lies in allowing them to become master.

The second bit of statesmanlike advice, easy to issue from the tenured halls of academe, is to try and take the long view in the formulation of economic policy. To the frustrated adviser, it often seems as if the politician's idea of the long run is about nine months. This is hardly surprising; to no one does Keynes's adage that "In the long run we are all dead" apply as aptly as to our elected officials. Since the president must risk his survival at the polls every four years, and our legislators every two or six years, one can hardly blame them for worrying more about the impact of a particular decision over the next six months or a year than about its implications for our economy a decade hence. The trouble is, there is great pressure on the president's economic advisers to develop the same myopia. Preoccupied during much of their 12-hour days and six-day weeks with putting out the urgent policy brushfires that constantly spring up all around them, they find it increasingly difficult to focus on the long-term implications of the policies they are recommending—or opposing. But they must persevere. Just as it is the function of the CEA to speak for the general economic interest in the face of pressures from a wide variety of special interest, so, I would argue, should they be the guardians of the future in the face of heavy pressures to focus on the immediate or short-run effects of alternative policy choices and let the long run take care of itself.

Finally, there is the need for perspective. Perhaps the best protection for the president and his advisers against promising too much and for the public against expecting or demanding too much as we jointly continue our pursuit of the economic grail, would be for all of us to keep in mind certain fundamental truths. These truths are not new, but they are easy to forget, and it is only recently that we have been forcibly reminded of them. The first is that scarcity is real. The second is that the United States is part of the rest of the world. And the third is that uncertainty is the essence of the human condition.

7

FULL RECOVERY
OR STAGNATION?
James Tobin

THE U.S. ECONOMY IN 1977:
A HANSEN-KEYNES DIAGNOSIS

It is a pleasure to join other former members of the CEA in this series of essays. What would I advise now? Since I'm not advising anybody now, I can be somewhat irresponsible. The title "Full Recovery or Stagnation?" is a deliberate steal. Those few readers who are of my generation, perhaps some younger scholars as well, will recognize the title of a book by Alvin Hansen of Harvard University, one of my teachers. Published in 1938 during the slow and incomplete recovery from the Great Depression, the book advocated expansionary fiscal policy to speed up recovery and restore full employment. Although our recent recession is nothing like the Great Depression, our problem today resembles the one Hansen wrote about. That is why I borrowed his title.

As the title suggests, I propose to argue for a Keynesian diagnosis of the present situation. Such a diagnosis is not popular these days. Forty years after the *General Theory of Employment, Interest, and Money* was published in 1936, it seems like old hat. But I do not apologize. I recognize that there are plenty of non-Keynesian problems facing the economy, plenty of structural problems, plenty of long-run supply problems. There always are. Maybe they are unusually numerous and difficult today—consider energy, environment, urban pathology, and so on. But stagnation in the sense of Hansen or Keynes will contribute nothing to the solution of long-run structural problems. Indeed full recovery would not prevent or delay the necessary solutions.

What is a Keynesian diagnosis of the current situation? It is essentially too little spending, deficient effective demand for goods and services. It's a most remarkable fact that many people, including economists, are extremely reluctant to accept so simple a diagnosis. They resist it very strongly. Consequently they are extremely reluctant to accept the obvious prescription, to step up aggregate demand for goods and services and labor, using well-known government policy instruments, fiscal policy and monetary policy.

Here you have a patient showing all the classical symptoms of simple malnutrition. The doctors stand around looking for esoteric maladies, sleeping sickness or atrophy of the stomach or bottlenecks in the alimentary canal. They refuse to admit that the old-fashioned classical malady could in fact exist. Some of them even say, to pursue the analogy in the spirit of Christian Science, that the patient reveals by his very emaciation that he prefers that state. Let him alone, especially because everybody knows that feeding him could only result in obesity.

The spring of 1977 begins the third year of recovery from the worst recession of postwar American economic history. The recession lasted about 15 months from the final quarter of 1973. In March 1975, the recovery started. Unemployment was 5 percent of the labor force in the winter of 1973–74. It rose sharply to 9 percent in the spring of 1975. After two years, it has not even recovered half the distance to its prerecession peak; unemployment in the spring of 1977 stands at 7.5 percent. The real GNP, the *volume* of production of goods and services, is still somewhat less than 3 percent above its prerecession peak. Although it's 9–10 percent above the trough in 1975, the United States has barely recovered the absolute volume of production of 1973–74.

Now that may not seem so bad. But let me remind the reader that par for this economy is an annual growth in real GNP of 3.5 percent per year; some say as much as 4 percent. That is the rate of growth necessary to absorb the normal increases in the labor force and in the productivity of labor. Had the United States been on that well-established postwar trend since the beginning of 1974, the GNP now would be 10 percent or 13 percent above what it was then, not just 3 percent.

Something on the same order is true of industrial production. You read in the newspaper that it grew by 1 percent between January and February 1977. But what you didn't read in the paper is that, even so, the industrial production index stands only 2 percent above what it was way back in 1973. It is not just labor that is in excess supply and unemployed; capital also is unemployed. The index of capacity utilization in industry shows that even by the spring of 1977, operating rates average around 80 percent. Back at the prerecession peak in 1973 operating rates were close to 90 percent, on the average 89 percent. They fell to 73 percent in the trough of the recession. The United States has less excess capacity in the spring of 1977, but there's still a lot of it, a lot of factories underutilized, machines idle, just like the men who used to run them.

Perhaps the principal disaster area at this time is the rate of investment by business firms in new plant and equipment, still 12 percent below in real value what it was before the recession. At the trough of the recession, it was down nearly 20 percent. Investment has recovered only a small part of the lost ground, in absolute terms. Normally it would have grown with the labor force and the size of the economy.

Why after two years of recovery is the economy still so depressed? The recovery started off pretty well in 1975. It was driven by a boost in consumption spending, stimulated by tax reductions and tax rebates. These were enacted in 1975 at the initiative of the Congress and reluctantly signed by President Gerald Ford. He had, until late in 1974, been under the mistaken impression that the main problem the country faced was inflation rather than recession. Subsequently, the driving force of the recovery, through early 1976, was inventory rebuilding, a common phenomenon in business-cycle upswings. During the recession itself, business inventories became excessive relative to depressed sales and production. During 1975, business firms ran off their excess inventories. When that process had gone on long enough and consumption spending was on the upswing again, then business began restocking. The rebuilding of inventories gave production a considerable boost, especially in early 1976. This follows a classic business-cycle pattern. But, in the later part of 1976, sales slowed considerably and production growth fell below the par of 3.5–4 percent necessary to absorb the increasing labor force and productivity. That is why the unemployment rate shot up again in late 1976.

The administration and many forecasters had been saying that business investment would keep the recovery going in late 1976 and 1977. That often happens in the second stage of a recovery, after the inventory boom peters out. But this time it didn't happen, and it still hasn't happened. Investment remains very weak.

IS UNEMPLOYMENT REALLY A PROBLEM?

This brief history sets the stage. The Carter administration has some interest in consolidating the recovery and assuring its continuation. I shall discuss current policies and proposals. But first I want to mention a number of arguments frequently advanced to explain away the whole problem I just described. These arguments represent what I earlier called the Christian Science diagnosis: There really isn't anything wrong. If the reader doesn't believe that people say that, all one has to do is read any issue of the *Wall Street Journal*, or for that matter quite a few issues of some professional economic journals. Or read, for example, the findings of what is known as the Shadow Open Market Committee, a group of monetarist economists who second-guess the Federal Reserve system periodically.

Let me go through a list of these arguments and comment on them. There are a number of current explanations for why unemployment doesn't really exist or at least why it isn't as high as the number, 7.5 percent, makes one think it is, or anyway makes me think it is. First, there is the idea that unemployment today is not really involuntary, that the labor force likes to be emaciated, like the patient I referred to in the beginning. Workers have revealed their preference for being unemployed by the fact that wages are not falling. If there really is excess supply, whether for labor or for fresh fish, economists *know* that the price must fall. But as we observe, wages continue to rise in the labor market, proving ipso facto that there is no involuntary unemployment. Now that is exactly the same doctrine that Keynes and Hansen confronted in the 1930s: Even when there is 25 percent unemployment, absence of rapid wage deflation shows the labor force must really like it that way. No need to do anything special about it.

For some economists, I am afraid, the idea that excess supply simply cannot persist is such a strong article of faith that it is virtually a tautology. If high unemployment persists for two or three years, and if they cannot reconcile it to the theory of competitive markets—well then, they are inclined to say it doesn't exist. Instead, what must have happened, in their view, is that voluntary or natural unemployment increased. But we know, as Keynes knew in the 1930s, that wage and price patterns are sticky. Those patterns don't change fast, and unemployed workers cannot make them change fast. Vast excess supply of labor and other resources persisted for more than a decade in the 1930s, and the same phenomenon on a smaller scale is occurring in the 1970s.

In the present situation, there are a number of variations on the theme that unemployment is really voluntary. The disadvantages of being unemployed have been reduced by unemployment compensation and other social benefits, notably food stamps. However, only half the unemployed actually receive unemployment compansation. Then there's the minimum wage, which may indeed contribute a certain amount of unemployment of teenagers and other young and unskilled workers. Another variant points to the changing demographic composition of the labor force: the increasing participation of women and teenagers relative to prime-age male adults with household responsibilities. Consequently we have a bunch of people without firm attachment to the labor force.

They keep on shifting voluntarily from one job to another. They are caught in the surveys in between jobs and increase the normal rate of unemployment. This shift can actually be calculated by looking at change in the composition of the labor force, and it is worth about 1 point in the unemployment rate compared to 1965, making 5 percent unemployment now the equivalent of 4 percent then.

The trouble with a number of these propositions is that they are refuted by statistics published for everyone to read. Consider the increase in unemployment between 1973 and now. The marginal unemployment, the difference between 5 and 7.5 percent, is mainly due to layoffs, not to voluntary quits. Almost half the people who are unemployed today lost their last jobs. They didn't quit, and they are not new entrants into the labor force. They were laid off. In normal times like 1973, that figure is around 38 percent. Moreover, the increase in unemployment was concentrated on prime workers, married men, experienced workers, male adults. These are the unemployment rates that have more than proportionately increased. For example, males over twenty: 3.2 percent in 1973, 6 percent in December 1976, 5.6 percent in January 1977; females over 20: 4.8 percent in 1973, 6.9 percent in the spring of 1977. On the other hand, teenagers' unemployment rose only from 14.5 to 18.5 percent, a relatively smaller increase than that of prime workers. Blacks' unemployment rate increased only from 9 to 12.5 percent between 1973 and early 1977, proportionately a much smaller increase than that for white males. It is true that unemployment falls disproportionately upon teenagers, blacks, and, to a lesser extent, adult women. But it's not true that the increase in unemployment was disproportionately concentrated on those groups.

It is, moreover, hardly credible that the preferences, habits, and mobility of the labor force suddenly changed and raised the natural rate of unemployment to 9 or 8 or 7 percent instead of 5 or 5.5 percent. There may be some steady trends in voluntary or frictional unemployment, but big jumps do not happen in 15 months. As for the argument that attributes the rise in unemployment to the liberalization of unemployment insurance, it was only after and in response to the spectacular increase in unemployment that benefits were raised and extended in duration.

A second major argument, which can can also be found every day in the *Wall Street Journal*, is that the problem is rapid growth in the labor force. Employment actually increased during the past two years of recovery. Indeed, the number of jobs exceeds, by 3 or 4 million, pre-recession levels. A new statistic has come into vogue, and one can read ad nauseum how this new statistic is more relevant than the old statistic, the unemployment rate. The new statistic is the employment ratio, the ratio of employment to the population of working age. This ratio, true enough, is high, historically high. The assertion is that we should not worry about the unemployment rate because the economy is employing a larger fraction of the people of working age. The implication is that one should not expect the economy to accommodate a rapid growth in the labor force. If people would stay home or go to school instead of looking for jobs, then we wouldn't have all this unemployment. And anyway, it's all because of those damned women. They come into the labor force at increasing rates, either becoming unemployed or displacing men.

This argument washes no better than the others. Yes, the labor force is growing rapidly, faster than the adult population. But the trend in labor-force participation is nothing new. Actually, in 1975 and 1976 the labor force grew less rapidly than in the three previous years. In 1972, 1973, and 1974, the number of persons employed or seeking work grew successively 2.4 million, 2.2 million, and 2.3 million. In 1975, it grew only 1.6 million. And in 1976, when we were hearing this complaint, how much did labor force grow? The answer is 2.1 million, not as many as have successfully been absorbed into employment in prosperous years in the past. The trend of labor-force participation of women is not new. It has been proceeding for two decades or longer, and it cannot be held responsible for the present high unemployment rate. Both women's lib and men's lib should resent the curious idea that women can get jobs only if men are displaced. There is no reason why the economy cannot create jobs to match the increased desire of the population to work.

It should also be noticed that there are inconsistencies among the arguments advanced to explain away the unemployment problem. On the one hand, too many people don't want to work; on the other hand, too many people do want to work.

CAPACITY AND INVESTMENT

I turn now to unemployment of capital capacity. It's pretty hard to argue that idle machine tools are voluntarily unemployed, that they would rather be searching for jobs or otherwise whiling away their time than working. That would be a rather anthropomorphic view of excess capacity. I haven't actually seen articles explaining away unemployment of capital as voluntary in the *Journal of Political Economy*, but I expect to. A less far-fetched point is that the economy is nearing bottlenecks, that the margins are really very small, and that much so-called excess capacity is obsolete. Now there has never been a business cycle trough, I suspect, at which one could not have found some bottlenecks looming ahead. They could have been found if one looked hard enough in 1933. If recovery must be delayed because in some sector utilization of capacity will be tightened before the rest of the economy has recovered, the United States would be doomed to stagnation.

The concern about bottlenecks now is the fear that some prices will rise. Americans are so paranoid about inflation these days that they can't tolerate the possibility that any particular commodity might rise in price, essential as that increase might be for the operation of the market system.

I am not counseling complacency about the adequacy of productive capacity. There has been, it seems, a slight, maybe more than slight, rise in the rate of unemployment of labor associated with any given rate of utilization of industrial capacity. That is a disturbing fact. If it is not corrected, it increases the difficulty of obtaining low levels of unemployment of labor without running into lots of bottlenecks. In fact, one of my objections to prolonged stagnation is the reinforcement of this trend. Bottleneck warnings will become a self-fulfilling prophecy. Stagnation weakens investment, and without normal investment capacity, limits are encountered with higher unemployment. In 1980, the inflation hawks who now say that 6 or 7 percent is as low a rate of unemployment as we can safely have, will tell us that it's 7 or 8 percent. The cause will be all the capacity we are losing in the meantime by following their policy prescriptions. It is a never-never-land impasse, catch-22. On the one hand, we're told, we can't expand the economy because we might run into some bottlenecks. On the other hand, businessmen see no incentive to expand capacity and eliminate the bottlenecks because they don't foresee the sales and output to justify new capacity.

Everyone deplores the current low rates of investment and worries about their implications both for the recovery and for the long run. But observers differ in their diagnoses why business investment is weak. One diagnosis is inadequacy of expected profits and sales, because businessmen are not sure how long or how strong this recovery will be. They don't see the need for future capacity as long as they have excess capacity. Relative to those expectations, the financial cost of capital is quite high. It is a striking fact that at current interest rates and equity prices, the bond and stock markets don't believe that the producing assets of U.S. corporations are worth the steel and cement they're made of. The ratio of the value of those securities to the underlying productive assets is less than one. The stock and bond markets say that the physical assets are worth only about 80 percent of what it would cost to rebuild them at current commodity prices and construction costs. Thus the financial climate is not favorable for investment. An indicative symptom is the 1977 decision of the IBM Corporation to use its cash to repurchase its own stock. At the present market price of the stock, that was the best thing they could do on behalf of their stockholders.

The foregoing is a straightforward explanation of the weakness of investment. But there are alternative diagnoses that, like the tortured attempts to explain away unemployment, evade the obvious deficiency of final demand. One hears a lot about government regulations, about Occupational Safety and Health Administration (OSHA) codes, about environmental restrictions, about the double taxation of corporate earnings, about political hostility to free enterprise. It certainly is remarkable how those impacts occurred so suddenly. None of those factors changed in recent years. They were all present before the recession, the same environmental restrictions, the same OSHA, the same double taxation, the same public attitudes. It is hard to see how they could suddenly have caused the collapse of business confidence, and during a Republican administration at that.

One regularity of business cycles is that these complaints recur. Their function is to prepare the way for additional tax concessions—for example, increases in the investment tax credit. Once the tax concessions are granted in recessions, they are generally permanent.

Another alleged reason for the weakness of investment is fear of accelerated inflation, inevitably followed by another recession. This is the first explanation in different guise. The pessimistic expectations really concern government policy. Businessmen are undoubtedly correct that bad news on the inflation front will result in restrictive Federal Reserve policy. The Fed's record in 1974 and Chairman Burns's public pronouncements certainly support these fears.

POLICY FOR FULL RECOVERY

How fast a recovery should the United States have? I remind the reader that par is 3.5 or 4 percent growth in production each year. And I ask the rhetorical question: How many years must America take to regain the ground it lost in 15 months? It has already taken two years, and the nation has not regained much ground. It's true that real GNP has been growing at an average 5 percent per year these last two years. But that's not really very high compared to par. As a matter of fact, a GNP growth rate of 5.5 percent, somewhat better than par, will reduce unemployment only by about 0.5 percent a year—a very slow process.

Go-slow recovery was the deliberate policy of the Ford administration and remains the deliberate policy of the Federal Reserve. The strategy is to reduce the stubborn inflation rate by sustaining high unemployment and excess capacity for the rest of the decade or longer. If inflation abatement takes precedence over every other objective, the policy makes some sense. Such thinking influences members of the Carter administration, too. They have been anxious not to propose a stimulus package so strong, and so different from what might have happened under the previous regime, as to cause worries in the financial and business community.

The 1977 Carter recovery package, as I understand it, has the following objectives and features. First, there is a quick one-shot $11 billion fiscal stimulus to be administered in 1977, in the not too distant future, the $50 per person payment.* One reason is to ensure against a further slowdown like the one in the last part of 1976. Second, the package provides continuing fiscal stimulus through 1978. One item is permanent income tax reduction, about $6 billion once it comes fully into effect. Third, the package includes direct expenditures on public works and jobs programs. These build up to about another $7 billion in 1978. Fourth, the administration has also asked for a two-point increase in the investment tax credit until 1980, and a modest tax incentive for employment.†

The total stimulus package amounts to some $15 billion in each of the two fiscal years 1977 and 1978. Most of it is temporary. Like the rebate, some expenditure programs will phase out. The administration does not wish to give tax revenues away permanently. The president has promised to balance the budget for fiscal year 1981. The promise is politically motivated, of course. But it also makes good economic sense. Once recovery is complete and business investment demand revives, federal deficits would absorb private saving that could better go into private capital formation. The Carter package is not large relative to the size of the economy. Compare the Kennedy-Johnson fiscal stimulus proposed in 1963 and enacted in 1964. This too was designed to pep up a sluggish recovery. Taxes were reduced $13 billion in an economy one-third the dollar size of the present economy. Relative to the GNP, the annual stimulus in the Carter package is less than half as large as the fiscal stimulus of 1964.

Although monetary policy receives much less public and congressional attention than fiscal proposals, it plays a crucial role in the strategy of recovery. Most of the fiscal stimulus is temporary, and recovery will not be complete when it is withdrawn after 1978. What will keep the recovery going? The natural answer is monetary policy. It is particularly important for the revival of investment. Beginning right now, the Federal Reserve should be preparing the ground for substantial improvement in private investment in 1978 and beyond. An investment revival is essential for the continuation of the recovery, as well as for meeting the long-run capital needs of the country.

The implications for monetary policy are two. One is psychological. The Federal Reserve should make clear that it will not choke off the

---

*President Carter withdrew this proposal in April.

†The increase in investment tax credit was also dropped, but a small employment incentive, in form different from the president's proposal, survived.

recovery but will let it proceed without significant credit tightening and increases in interest rates. Then businessmen can plan and expand capacity with confidence that sales and output will justify investment decisions made now and executed next year or later. The second monetary recommendation is to improve the financial climate for investment promptly and directly. The Federal Reserve should lower interest rates now. These actions would be a tonic for the stock and bond markets. Higher prices of corporate securities signify reduction in the cost of funds for financing investment. The ratio of securities' market values to capital replacement costs, which I described above, should be pushed above 1 again. Then companies like IBM will no longer find that the way to benefit their stockholders is to buy back stock. They will find instead that they can do their stockholders good by investing in productive capital.

The present policies of the Federal Reserve are very likely inconsistent with this scenario. The Federal Reserve has announced 1977's targets for their rate of growth of monetary aggregates M1, M2, M3, M7, M19, and so on. And these targets really are pretty stingy. Their target for M1, for the year is between 4.5 and 6.5 percent, and for M2, which includes commercial bank time and savings deposits as well as currency and demand deposits, between 7 and 9.5 percent.* Now if production grows at 5 to 6 percent and inflation continues at 5 or 6 percent, the monetary system will have to accommodate a growth of money value GNP of 10 to 12 percent. Maybe the Fed's monetary growth rates will do that. Maybe not. In the last two years, similarly modest growth rates of money stock sufficed for comparably larger growth in dollar GNP, while interest rates actually declined on balance. It was mostly luck. The velocity of money rose sharply and unexpectedly. There is certainly no guarantee that such good luck will continue. Without it, interest rates will rise, and the recovery will be imperiled.

This prospect exemplifies a serious political problem. Congress and the president make fiscal policy; they determine the budget. Their budget in 1977 aims at, and assumes, a certain path for the economy, about 6 percent real growth during the year. But whether they can actually achieve this goal does not depend entirely or even principally upon what they do with the fiscal instruments they control, taxes and expenditures. It also depends upon Burns and his colleagues at the Fed. They have the last word, and their monetary decisions month after month can offset, even nullify, the policies of the Congress and the administration. The United States certainly needs a policy-making mechanism that holds both the monetary and fiscal policies to the same economic objectives and

---

*As announced by Chairman Burns on May 3, 1977.

assigns to each its proper role in achieving them. It makes no sense to have a team of two horses pulling in opposite directions.

By now I have indicated what I would advise on these fronts: even a larger fiscal package than the Carter administration proposed, and at the same time a low-interest-rate monetary policy to encourage revival of investment later in 1977 and in 1978. In addition, I strongly believe, the United States needs public assurance from Chairman Burns that the Federal Reserve will support the same real targets of economic growth to which the Congress and the administration are committed.

I would not ask the Federal Reserve to underwrite higher rates of inflation. I would ask it to explain that expansion of money stock in this kind of economy, with a lot of excess capacity and unemployment, will expand production and employment without accelerating the rate of inflation. If the United States overshoots and tried to reduce unemployment below 5 percent, the inflation rate might very well rise. But there is a lot of room on the high side of that rate. Go-slow policies remind me of someone starting on an auto trip on an interstate highway from, say, Kalamazoo to Detroit, remembering that there are stoplights in Detroit, and therefore going 20 miles an hour on the outskirts of Kalamazoo. Arthur Burns will have time to slow the rate of monetary growth down before we get to Detroit. And, if he explains that to his admiring and influential public, then maybe he can undo the damage he has done by the doctrine that any higher rate of monetary growth is per se inflationary.

INFLATION AND INCOMES POLICIES

Events of the past ten years have bequeathed the United States a persistent underlying inflation of 5 to 6 percent per year. I refer to the basic wage-price patterns of the U.S. industrial economy. One should not, President Carter should not, Arthur Burns should not, get excited about "noise" in the inflation statistics, movements up or down from month to month, due to coffee, OPEC, sugar, orange juice, or other commodities. It is better to keep one's eyes on the underlying rate of inflation. This is geared to the rate of wage inflation, running around 7.5 to 8 percent per year, down from 9 percent a couple of years ago. The decrease can be attributed to the recession and to the policy that brought the recession. It takes a long time and a lot of unemployment for meager results, but it does work. The current wage inflation is consistent with our 5.5–6 percent price inflation. That is evident if one merely subtracts from the wage inflation the normal growth of labor productivity, 2.5–3 percent per year.

Why does the United States experience wage and price inflation at the current rates? History provided those rates of inflation. Suppose some economists arrive from a Rip Van Winkle sleep or from outer space. They don't know the country's inflation rate, and I ask them to guess it. I give them hints about unemployment, excess capacity, all those things. I ask them what would be the rate of inflation in an economy of that description. There's no way they could answer. The rate of inflation has no systematic or predictable relationship to the contemporary real economy. It could be 1 percent, it could be 12 percent, so far as those objective facts about the economy are concerned. It happens that a rocky history, beginning in 1966 with the Vietnam War, has left the United States with the stubborn inflation it has today.

What are the options for the United States with respect to this inflation? One option is the Ford-Burns reaction: We must "whip inflation now," and we will put the economy through years of stagnation if necessary. This is a slow process, and terribly costly. The difference between 7.5 percent unemployment and 5 percent unemployment, those 2.5 points of unemployment, makes a difference in GNP, real GNP, of about $150 billion a year. That is a lot of production, more than the whole defense budget. The extra output and income would greatly augment wages, profits, consumption, investment, and tax revenues. The Ford-Burns go-slow policy has cost the United States dearly. It has gained it very little in inflation abatement. Indeed such a policy may in some sense be counterproductive in the long run. Earlier, I referred to the possibility that stagnation could so discourage capital formation and capacity expansion that the economy would become inflationary at even higher rates of unemployment than it would today.

A second strategy would be to let bygones be bygones, accept the ongoing rate of inflation, and bring the economy back to something like 5.5 to 5 percent unemployment without appreciable change in the basic rate of inflation. This strategy would minimize further loss of output but avoid further acceleration of inflation. Since the unemployment rate would still be high, especially among disadvantaged groups, the United States would simultaneously undertake direct employment policies. Their aim would be further reduction of the unemployment rate than can be achieved by fiscal and monetary policies alone.

A third route would be direct attack on the ongoing rate of inflation itself. The generic term "incomes policies" covers everything from voluntary guideposts for wage and price behavior to full-blown wage and price controls. When most noneconomists are confronted with the inflation and unemployment dilemma and they are told that there's no way to have acceptable levels of both at the same time, they will just not believe it. They say there *must* be a third way out. They instinctively think there must be a way of controlling wages and prices that would avoid the painful choice of evils. It's noteworthy that those who are most committed to the eradication of inflation, most committed to doing it by prolonged stagnation, are completely unreceptive to the idea that there is any other way out. They like the idea that the cure is painful. It's better for you. They are ideologically opposed to any government interference with the market system. I think it's hard to justify their view on any pragmatic, cost-benefit analysis. On one occasion I told a group—this is a joke that will mean something only to professional economists—that it takes a heap of Harberger triangles to fill an Okun gap. Translated, this means that the losses of national output due to distortions in the allocation of resources by guideposts or wage-price policies of various kinds are small in relation to the $150 billion a year lost by running the economy at high levels of unemployment.

Business leaders and union spokesmen are also very adamant in their opposition to incomes policies. I think that we need some imaginative and innovative policies. Such divergent economists as Henry Wallich (my former Yale colleague now on the Federal Reserve Board, once on the Eisenhower Council of Economic Advisers) and University of Pennsylvania Professor Sidney Weintraub have both made a proposal deserving of much more consideration than it has received. They suggested that we **use good free-market incentive principles to induce noninflationary behavior. The idea is to increase profits tax on companies that give wage** increases averaging above a designated guidepost. For example, suppose the guidepost for wage increases this year was 5 percent. If a company gives more than 5 percent, then for every point it exceeds 5 percent it pays an extra point on its corporate profits tax. One could use a carrot as well as a stick. If the firm does better than the guidepost, restrains wage increases to less than the 5 percent, then the government will give both employer and employees a proportional rebate of payroll taxes. That is only one of a number of devices—gimmicks, if you like—that have been proposed. These are not full and rigid wage and price controls, but they have more bite than advisory guideposts. They all have problems. But their great advantage is that they might be an alternative to the defeatist view that the only way to lick the inflation problem is to run the economy with a tremendous amount of unemployment and lost production for many years.

I hope that the Carter administration and Congress will be adventurous on this front, and I hope they will follow policies for rapid and complete recovery. To succeed, they will need to obtain the cooperation of the Federal Reserve, which is in the last analysis responsible to Congress.

111

Mills, Wilbur, 49; bill, 49
minimum wages, 3, 12, 15, 100
monetarism, 69
monetary policy, 3, 4, 11, 19, 27,
    33, 35, 36, 38, 43, 56, 63, 65,
    70, 71, 72, 74, 98, 105, 106, 108
Morgenthau, Henry, 22
Mosca, Ugo, 54
Moynihan, Patrick, 51
multinational corporations (MNCs),
    32
Murray bill, 27

National Planning Association, 27-28
National Planning, commission of,
    89
National Security Council, 52
negotiable orders of withdrawal, 72
New Deal, 21
New International Economic Order,
    4, 17, 31, 41, 94
New York City taxi cabs, 12
Nixon, Richard M. (administration),
    45, 52, 53, 54, 56, 59, 62
Nourse, Edwin G., 28

Old Age and Survivors Insurance, 42
    (See also, Social Security)
Okun, Arthur, 77, 109
OPEC (Organization of Petroleum
    Exporting Countries), 17, 31, 33,
    80, 90, 92, 93, 107
Organization for Economic Coopera-
    tion and Development (OECD), 63
OSHA (Occupational Safety and
    Health Administration), 104

planning, federal, 4, 5, 25, 27, 40,
    41, 42, 43, 89, 90, 91
President's Council of Economic
    Advisers (See, Council of Eco-
    nomic Advisers)
productivity, 14, 33, 34, 74, 75, 83,
    84, 85-86, 98, 99, 107
profits, corporate, 3, 13
protectionism, 49, 50, 56, 61
Public Works Administration (PWA),
    23

pump priming, 22

quantity theory (See, monetarism)

rationing, 24
Reuss, Henry, 48, 57, 58, 60, 62
Roosevelt, Franklin D., 21, 22, 23

Samuelson, Paul, 48
Say, J. B., 20
Schmidt, Wilson, 50
Schultz, Charles, 67
Schweizer, Pierre-Paul, 61
Shadow Open Market Committee,
    100
Sherman Antitrust Act, 20
Smith, Adam, 18
Smithsonian Agreement, 59
Social Security, 84, 87; Act, 23
Soviet Union, 48, 57
special drawing rights (SDRs), 4,
    48, 60
Special Representative for Trade
    Negotiations, 8
Spence bill, 27
stagflation, 5, 79, 81, 83
stagnation, 102, 103, 108, 109
State Department, U.S., 9, 52
St. Louis equation (See, Federal
    Reserve Bank of St. Louis)
swap arrangements, 4, 47-48, 60

telecommunications policy, 8
Tobin, James, 2, 3, 6
Townsend, Francis E., 23
Trade Expansion Act, 49
transfer payments, 42, 44, 66, 87
Treasury, U.S., 19, 27, 38, 50,
    51, 52, 54, 58, 63; secretary
    of, 22, 56, 62
Truman, Harry S., 7, 19, 27, 29, 94

undistributed profits tax, 22
unemployment (types), excessive
    cost increase, 35; frictional,
    35, 38, 73, 101; inadequate de-
    mand, 35; structural, 35, 38;
    voluntary, 36, 38, 100, 101

112

unemployment compensation, 6, 95, 100, 101
unemployment data, 81, 100, 101
unemployment duration, 15
unemployment insurance, 42
unions, labor, 49
United Auto Workers (UAW), 89
United Kingdom (U.K.), 15 (See also, England)
United Nations, 29, 31

Vanek, Jaroslav, 48
Virginia Polytechnic Institute, 50
Volcker, Paul (group), 52, 53, 54, 55, 56, 57, 62

wage-price guidelines, 26

Wall Street Journal, 100, 101
Wallich, Henry, 50, 109
Watergate, 52
Weintraub, Sidney, 109
Western Michigan University, 6
Whitman, Marina v. N., 2, 3, 5-6, 52
Willett, Thomas, 50, 51
Wisconsin State Tax Commission, 19
Wonnacott, Paul, 52
Woodcock, Leonard, 89
Works Progress Administration (WPA), 23
World Bank, 93

Yale University, 50, 109

ABOUT THE EDITOR AND CONTRIBUTORS

WERNER SICHEL is Professor of Economics at Western Michigan University. He has served as a consultant to several business firms, consumer groups, and law firms. Dr. Sichel is past President of the Economics Society of Michigan. In 1968–69 he was a Fulbright-Hays Senior Lecturer at the University of Belgrade in Yugoslavia. He is a frequent contributor to various business and economics journals, especially in the field of industrial organization. He is the author of *Basic Economic Concepts*, 2d edition (1977), and the editor of *Industrial Organization and Public Policy: Selected Readings* (1967), *Antitrust Policy and Economic Welfare* (1970), *Public Utility Regulation: Change and Scope* (1975), *The Economic Effects of Multinational Corporations* (1975), and *Salvaging Public Utility Regulation* (1976).

PAUL W. McCRACKEN is a well-known scholar and practitioner in the fields of economics and finance. He served as Member of the President's Council of Economic Advisers from 1956 to 1959 and then returned to the Council at the beginning of 1969 to serve for three more years as its Chairman. Dr. McCracken is now Chairman of an international committee of economists commissioned by the Organization for Economic Cooperation and Development (OECD) in Paris to make recommendations on economic policy. Winner of awards and author of many papers and monographs on economic and financial policy, Dr. McCracken is a member of several professional societies and a director of several corporate boards. He has lectured throughout the world and participated in national economic commissions, task forces, and advisory boards.

ROY BLOUGH is a well-known economist who has worked primarily in the fields of taxation and international business. He served as a member of the President's Council of Economic Advisers from 1950 to 1952. He has also been Director of Tax Research in the U.S. Treasury Department as well as Assistant to the Secretary of the Treasury. From 1952 to 1955 he was Principal Director of the Department of Economic Affairs, The United Nations Secretariat. Dr. Blough has taught at Manchester College, The University of Cincinnati, The University of Chicago, and for the 15 years before his retirement at Columbia University. At the Graduate School of Business, Columbia University, he was S. Sloan Colt Professor of Banking and International Business. Dr. Blough was President of the Midwest Economic Association, Vice-President of the American Economic Association, and Director of International Finance of the American Finance Association. He has served as Editor of *Bulletin of the National Tax Association* and *National Tax Journal*, as well as a member of the Editorial Board of *International Organization* and *Columbia Journal of World Business*. He is the author of several books and many scholarly articles. He has frequently presented testimony before various Congressional committees.

HENDRIK S. HOUTHAKKER is Professor of Economics at Harvard University, where he has taught since 1960. His areas of interest include economic theory, econometrics, and economic policy. He has applied econometric techniques to a wide variety of problems, including consumer demand in this country and abroad, international economic relations, and commodity markets. In 1969, President Nixon named Professor Houthakker as one of the three members of his Council of Economic Advisers; he served in this capacity until July 1971. Previously, he had served on the staff of President Johnson's Council of Economic Advisers. He is currently a consultant to several government agencies and a member of thr National Commission on Supplies and Shortages. Professor Houthakker was born in Amsterdam, the Netherlands, and completed his graduate work at the University of Amsterdam. Prior to joining the Harvard faculty, he taught at Stanford University (1954–60) and was Visiting Professor at the University of Tokyo, at MIT, and at Harvard. Earlier, he had conducted economic research at Cambridge University and was on the research staff of the Cowles Commission for Economic Research at the University of Chicago. Dr. Houthakker is the author of *The Analysis of Family Budgets* and *Consumer Demand in the United States, 1929–1970*. He has also written numerous articles in economic journals. Professor Houthakker received the American Economic Association's John Bates Clark medal in 1963. He was a Vice-President of the AEA in 1972. He is a Fellow of the Econometric Society, of which he was President in 1967.

JAMES S. DUESENBERRY is Chairman of the Department of Economics at Harvard University, where he has taught for the past three decades. He received both undergraduate and graduate degrees from the University of Michigan. Before joining the Harvard faculty he taught for a brief time at the Massachusetts Institute of Technology. Professor Duesenberry was a Fulbright Fellow at Cambridge University as well as a Ford Research Professor. From 1970 to 1975 he served as Chairman of the Board of Directors of the Federal Reserve Bank of Boston. In February

1966, President Lyndon Johnson named Professor Duesenberry to be one of the three members of his Council of Economic Advisers; he served in this capacity until June 1968. Dr. Duesenberry is the author of many books, including *Income Saving and the Theory of Consumer Behavior*, *Business Cycles and Economic Growth*, and *Money and Credit: Impact and Control*. He has also written a large number of essays and chapters in books. His scholarly articles have appeared in many economic journals including *The American Economic Review*, *Review of Economics and Statistics*, *Quarterly Journal of Economics*, *Econometrica*, and *Journal of Finance*.

MARINA v.N. WHITMAN is a Distinguished Public Service Professor of Economics at the University of Pittsburgh, were she has taught since the early 1960s. She received a B.A. degree from Radcliffe College and M.A. and Ph.D. degrees from Columbia University. In addition she has been the recipient of eight honorary Doctorates. Professor Whitman served on the editorial boards of *The American Economic Review* and *Foreign Policy*, is a Senior Adviser to the Brookings Panel on Economic Activity, and an adjunct Scholar of the American Enterprise Institute. She is a member of the Board of Overseers of Harvard University and a member of the Advisory Council of the Department of Economics of Princeton University. From March 1972 to August 1973, Dr. Whitman served as a member of the Council of Economic Advisers. Prior to that time she was a Senior Staff Economist for the Council of Economic Advisers and a member of the National Price Commission. Dr. Whitman is a Director of Manufacturers Hanover Trust, Westinghouse Electric Corporation, Marcor Corporation, and the Proctor & Gamble Company. Professor Whitman is the author of a large number of books, monographs, and articles. She has prepared several studies in international finance and economics published by Princeton University. Her articles have appeared in economic journals including *The American Economic Review*, *Journal of Finance*, and *Quarterly Journal of Economics*.

JAMES TOBIN is Sterling Professor of Economics at Yale University, where he has taught for over 25 years. For the past three years he has been Chairman of the Department. For six years he served as Director of the Cowles Foundation for Research in Economics at Yale. Professor Tobin holds A.B., M.A., and Ph.D. degrees from Harvard University and honorary doctorates from Dartmouth College, The University of Illinois, and Syracuse University. Dr. Tobin is a Past President of The American Economic Association and of the Econometric Society. He received the American Economic Association's John Bates Clark medal in 1955. From January 1961 to July 1962, Dr. Tobin served as a member of the Council of

Economic Advisers. He has also been a consultant to the Board of governors of the Federal Reserve System, the U.S. Treasury, the Office of Emergency Planning, the Ford Foundation, the Brookings Institution, and Harvard and MIT universities. Professor Tobin is the author or co-author of several books including *The American Business Creed* (1956), *National Economic Policy* (1966), *Essays in Economics* vol. 1 (1971) and vol. 2 (1975), and *The New Economics One Decade Older* (1974). His articles—about 150 of them—have appeared in leading economic journals including *The American Economic Review*, *Quarterly Journal of Economics*, *Review of Economics and Statistics*, *Review of Economic Studies*, *Economic Journal*, *Econometrica*, *Journal of Political Economy*, *Journal of Finance*, and *Economica*. He has also written for *The New Republic*, *Challenge*, *Fortune*, *The Public Interest*, *The Washington Post*, and *The New York Times*.

ASSOCIATION SYSTEM OF THE EUROPEAN COMMUNITY
Jacqueline D. Matthews

*FOREIGN TRADE AND U.S. POLICY: The Case
for Free International Trade
Leland B. Yeager
David G. Tuerck

THE FUTURE OF INTERNATIONAL ECONOMIC
ORGANIZATIONS
edited by
Don Wallace, Jr.
Helga Escobar

THE POLITICAL ECONOMY OF EAST-WEST TRADE
Connie M. Friesen

WORLD MONETARY DISORDER: National Policies vs.
International Imperatives
edited by
Patrick M. Boarman
David G. Tuerck

*Also available in paperback as a PSS Student Edition.